MARILYN TURK

Lighthouse Devotions

52 Inspiring Lighthouse Stories

Compiled and written by Marilyn Turk

ISBN: 978-1-959788-20-1

Dedication

This book is dedicated to my dear husband, Chuck, who has patiently supported me through this undertaking, by traveling to see lighthouses with me, encouraging me and reminding me that the inspiration for these devotions came from God to help others see His light.

Contents

Introduction

Big Sable Point Lighthouse, MI, photo by Chuck Turk

There's something about lighthouses. Something that draws us, inspires us, fills us with awe. Regal, strong, commanding, and sure—they evoke a sense of stately respect. Usually situated apart from the rest of civilization, they serve as isolated sentinels of the water, standing guard over their appointed domain.

To some people, lighthouses represent strength and stability, to others beauty and mystery, and still others hope and peace. They were created to protect, guide, and warn mariners of potential dangers. Even through violent storms, they remained steadfast at their post, faithful towers shining their beacons out upon the water. We ascribe human characteristics to these structures, respectful of their commitment and resolution.

But without keepers, these lighthouses could not serve the purpose for which they were built. Originally, men and women took great care of these structures—climbing spiral staircases, often carrying heavy buckets of oil to keep the lanterns lit at night, cleaning and polishing the lenses during the day to help the light shine brightly and sounding the fog horns when visibility was poor. These dedicated people were the true heroes of the lighthouses. They were the ones who brought the towers to life and gave them their dependability, sometimes at great risk and discomfort to themselves. The keepers were the real eyes of the lighthouse, searching for those in need, at risk, or in danger.

A lighthouse lover myself, I couldn't help but notice the connection between lighthouses and verses in the Bible. As I read these stories about lighthouses, Bible verses that related would come to mind. I researched the Bible for the word "light," and found it listed 335 times. In fact, the third verse in the Bible is "Let there be light." Light represents good, truth, clarity, revelation, and hope. It shows the way, reveals the dangers, and guides us. Lighthouses, then, are physical symbols of spiritual truths, hence the title of this book— "Lighthouse Devotions."

These stories are historical fiction. While most of these devotions are based on actual events, some have been enhanced by fictional dialogue or names, and some are based on events that happened at many lighthouses, but not a specific event at a specific location.

I hope you'll be blessed, entertained, enlightened, and inspired by these devotional stories. May God bless your journey and shed light on your path.

"Your word is a lamp to my feet and a light to my path." Psalm 119:105

Marilyn Turk

The Lighthouse Universal

Tourlitis Lighthouse, Greece, photo by Delores Reyes Pergiouda, courtesy of
Lighthouse Digest magazine

There are over 15,000 lighthouses in the world. To visit every one of them would take over forty years seeing one a day. On every continent in the world, from North America to South America, Europe to

3

Australia, Africa to Asia, and even one in Antarctica, lighthouses stand guard to protect mariners from danger. Virtually every country with large bodies of water has lighthouses – near oceans, lakes, rivers and bays. There are over a hundred along the Great Lakes alone.

From the first known lighthouse built in 240 B.C., men have built lighthouses on their shores. They have been constructed of a variety of materials such as wood, stone, or metal in assorted shapes like round, square or multi-sided. Their heights too, range from towers atop single-story houses such as the Cedar Key Light in Florida, to the tallest light in Saudi Arabia that tops 400 feet.

Water covers over seventy percent of the earth's surface and has been a means of transporting people and materials for thousands of years. For centuries, mariners all over the world have shared a universal need for direction to travel safely through the numerous bodies of water. Lighthouses served as their guides, their symbols of safety and direction.

We share the need for another light as well – that divine light that offers protection and guidance as we travel our lifetime journeys. No matter where we are, the light of God is available to all who seek it. He can turn our darkness into light if we let that light shine into our lives.

If I rise on the wings of the dawn, if I settle on the far side of the sea, even there your hand will guide me, your right hand will hold me fast.

If I say, Surely the darkness will hide me and the light become night around me, even the darkness will not be dark to you; the night will shine like the day, for darkness is as light to you. Psalm 139:9-12

Reflections

Have you ever gone through dark times? Did you ask for God's light to guide you through them?

Beacon Briefs

Tourlitis Lighthouse, Greece

Tourlitis, a unique lighthouse built in 1887 on a solitary rock off the coast of Andros Island, Greece, was bombed during World War II, then rebuilt afterwards. It has no keeper's quarters, and its steps are cut into the rock. The lighthouse marks the entrance to the harbor of Andros Chora, a popular port for today's cruise ships. Tourlitis was the first Greek lighthouse to be automated.

Legacy of a Lighthouse

Lighthouse of Alexandria, courtesy of Lighthouse Digest magazine

Pharology – is it the study of pharaohs? Sounds like it, doesn't it?

However, the word comes from "pharos," a Greek word meaning lighthouse, and refers to the first lighthouse known in history.

The Lighthouse of Alexandria was built on the island of Pharos at Alexandria, Egypt, between 280 and 247 B.C. during the reign of Ptolemy II to guide mariners into the harbor. At a height of approximately 400 feet, it was one of the tallest man-made structures in the world for hundreds of years and is known as one of the Seven Wonders of the Ancient World.

Made from huge blocks of stone, interlocked and sealed with molten lead to protect against water, the tower had three levels. The lowest level was square, then atop that was a smaller octagonal section, and on top of that was an even smaller circular section. At the very top was a mirror which reflected sunlight during the day, while a wood-burning fire provided light at night.

In the writings of Julius Caesar, Josephus, and even Chinese historians, the Lighthouse of Alexandria was mentioned as a prominent feature in the world while it stood. Its image and design have been preserved and copied in buildings and artwork for centuries since, even though the structure is now gone, a victim of earthquakes. Yet perhaps its main legacy is the word it conceived – *pharology* – or the study of lighthouses.

Like the other wonders of the world, the Alexandria Lighthouse has faded into history, its glory a thing of the past. We marvel at what man has made, even when we know it will not last. But daily, we see wonders God has created – beautiful sunsets, marvelous animals, stunning landscapes. These are wonders we often overlook, and yet they are part of the legacy God has left us.

"Many, LORD my God, are the wonders you have done, the things you planned for us. None can compare with you; were I to speak and tell of your deeds, they would be too many to declare." Psalm 40:5

Reflections

What are some of God's wonders you can thank him for?

Beacon Briefs

Lighthouse of Alexandria, Egypt

The Pharos Lighthouse was damaged by earthquakes until only the lower level remained. In 1480, the Sultan of Egypt built a medieval fort at the site using pieces of the fallen tower. Ruins of the lighthouse were discovered in the Alexandria harbor in 1994.

Two symbols – One Hope

Blackistone Lighthouse, Maryland

For many people throughout the world and the ages, lighthouses represent a variety of things. A sailor seeking safe passageway through dangerous waters welcomed the sight of a lighthouse to guide the way. It not only told him where he was but also warned him of danger. For some, the sight of a lighthouse gave them relief that land was near, a sign that their long and often perilous journey was coming to an end. It was a symbol of hope, strength, stability, as well as a symbol of security and reliability.

The cross is another symbol representing many things to many people. Where once an instrument of torture, it is now used around the world to commemorate the supreme sacrifice of Jesus, that sacrifice we recognize especially at Easter. It too, represents strength—spiritual strength, as well as stability, security, and reliability—characteristics Christ demonstrated in His love for us as He accepted the pain of the cross for our salvation.

Each lighthouse has a place in history and the lives it saved. However, those life-saving events were temporary. The salvation the cross represents, though, is eternal. For those seeking a true, life-changing experience, they must accept the spiritual cross of Jesus, the only everlasting symbol of hope.

"But he was pierced for our transgressions, he was crushed for our iniquities; the punishment that brought us peace was upon him, and by his wounds we are healed." Isaiah 53:5

Reflections

Why is hope important? What symbol means hope to you?

Beacon Briefs

Blackistone Lighthouse, Maryland

The Blackistone Island Lighthouse, built on St. Clement's Island in the Potomac River in 1851, was maintained and operated by the island's owner, Dr. Joseph McWilliams, his son, and then his daughter Josephine, who ran it until her death in 1912. Her four children were born and raised on the island where they all took part in the maintenance of the lighthouse.

The Hope of Grace

Longstone Lighthouse, United Kingdom, Photo by Steven Winter, courtesy of *Lighthouse Digest* magazine

September 7, 1838
Longstone Lighthouse, UK

Grace! Wake up! I need you to help me tie things down!" Lightkeeper William Darling gently shook his sleeping daughter.

Grace struggled to open her eyes, then heard the alarm in his voice and remembered her older brother wasn't home to help. Sixteen-year-old Grace jumped out of bed,

15

threw on some clothes, and hurried to follow her father down the lighthouse steps.

The waves were rising higher as they worked quickly to secure everything, including their fishing boat.

"That's done," Father said as they tied the last knot. "All we can do now is hope and pray the storm doesn't tear everything away."

Even though it was still before daylight, Grace couldn't go back to sleep. Instead, she stood by her third-story bedroom window, watching the storm grow furious outside. As sunlight grayed the sky, she thought she saw a large black shape on a small island called Big Harcar Rock. Was it a shipwreck? She ran to get her father.

"Father! I believe there's a shipwrecked out there!"

The two grabbed a telescope and searched the rocks for signs of life.

"Poor souls. Looks like the ship broke in half and only the bow is left. Father shook his head. "I don't believe anyone survived, Grace."

Grace refused to give up hope and continued to stare out the window, watching for movement. Around 7:00 in the morning, Grace saw activity on the rocks. There were survivors!

Once again, she ran to get her father. "I saw survivors! Please, we must go get them!"

"Grace, the sea is too treacherous to attempt it. Our boat might capsize in these waves."

But Grace was already down the stairs and headed for the boat. "Father, we can do this! We must try!"

He joined her, calculating the only way to access the rocks was to make a circuitous approach and use the tides to help them. With tremendous physical effort, he and Grace approached the rock, finding nine survivors – one woman and eight men—too many to take at once. So they took the woman first with two of the weakest men, plus two strong crewmen to help row the boat back. Once those people were safely deposited at the lighthouse, the keeper went back for the other four, rescuing all nine.

Word spread quickly of Grace Darling's bravery and determination to save the survivors, and the country hailed her as a public hero. Grace, however, refused to take credit for her actions, instead declaring the rescue was not due to her own efforts but the power of God. That power lay not only in her physical strength, but also in the hope she held onto for others to live.

"May our Lord Jesus Christ himself and God our Father, who loved us and by his grace gave us eternal encouragement and good hope, encourage your hearts and strengthen you in every good deed and word." 2 Thessalonians 2:16-17

Reflections

Do you ever feel overwhelmed and weak? What might you accomplish with God's enabling power?

Beacon Briefs

Longstone Lighthouse – United Kingdom

Longstone Lighthouse, established in 1826, is on one of the Farne Islands, six miles off the coast of mainland England, making it a very isolated location for its keepers and their families. Severe storms often forced the lighthouse occupants into the upper rooms of the tower where they sought refuge from enormous waves which covered the living quarters.

A Higher Perspective

Cape Hatteras, North Carolina, photo courtesy of The Lighthouse People

In the 1800's, the area of the ocean bordering the Outer Banks, North Carolina, had so many shipwrecks, it became known as the "Graveyard of the Atlantic." The danger was caused by Diamond Shoals, shallow sandbars that extend fourteen miles from the shore.

To solve the problem, a taller lighthouse was built in 1870 to replace the existing one. Called the Cape Hatteras Lighthouse, it became the tallest lighthouse in America with a beacon visible twenty miles from shore warning ships they were nearing the dangerous area.

From the top of the lighthouse, the keeper could look down and see how far out the shallow waters were. From his higher viewpoint, he could see the dangers the ships couldn't see.

Do you ever wish you could look down on your life from a higher perspective and see the whole picture? Many times, we can't see our way out of the situations we're in. All we see are the problems. We wish we could see our way clear and find the path to safety and peace.

I'm thankful that God has that higher perspective. He can see everything— the past, the present, the future. He warns us about the dangers in our paths, if we just pay attention to His guiding light.

"From heaven the Lord looks down and sees all mankind; from his dwelling place he watches all who live on earth— he who forms the hearts of all, who considers everything they do." Psalm 33:13-15

Reflections

Would you like to see your life from God's perspective? What could He see that you cannot? Ask Him to show you.

Beacon Briefs

Cape Hatteras, North Carolina

By 1970, beach erosion had brought the water within 120 feet of the lighthouse, so the National Park Service determined the structure would not survive another decade. After years of failed attempts to prevent further erosion, in an outstanding achievement by the American Society of Civil Engineers, the tall lighthouse was raised six feet off its base and carefully moved, in five-foot increments, along a roadway constructed for that purpose, arriving at its new and present location half a mile inland.

Spiders, Sparkplugs and Skeletons

Thomas Point Shoal Light, Chesapeake Bay, Maryland, photo courtesy of The Lighthouse People

What do you envision when you think of a lighthouse?

A tall, white, smooth cone like the Cape Florida Lighthouse?

Or perhaps an octagonal brick tower like the Old Cape Henry Lighthouse in Virginia?

Maybe a pyramid-style building come to mind like the East Quoddy Lighthouse in New Brunswick, Canada.

These styles of lighthouses are the most common and most photographed. But other styles exist as well.

The screw-pile-style was usually built over water by drilling pilings into the bottom of the sand or mud. The lighthouse was then built on a platform on the pilings, which resemble legs, hence the name "spiders." An

23

example of this style is the Thomas Point Lighthouse in Chesapeake Bay, Maryland.

A sparkplug lighthouse? Such a nickname is given to a caisson-style lighthouse. These lighthouses, a cheaper alternative to the screw-pile styles, rested on concrete or metal caissons. The result gave the lighthouse the appearance of a sparkplug. Goose Rocks Lighthouse, off the coast of Maine, is typical of this style.

Skeleton lighthouses resemble oil derricks. They consist mainly of an open, metal framework with a central staircase. More suited for open, exposed waters, such lighthouses were first built on the reefs of the Florida Keys. The Sombrero Key Light is an example of this style.

Although different styles are necessary for different conditions, but all these lighthouses serve the same function – to guide mariners to safety and warn them of danger.

The Bible says believers have been given different gifts such as wisdom, hospitality, service and giving. One person has one gift, another person has something else. We're not all alike, yet we all serve the same God.

"There are different kinds of gifts, but the same Spirit distributes them. There are different kinds of service, but the same Lord. There are different kinds of working, but in all of them and in everyone it is the same God at work." 1 Corinthians 12:4-6

Reflections

What kind of lighthouse would you be—a spider, a sparkplug, a skeleton, or another style? The style doesn't matter, as long as your light shines.

Beacon Briefs

Thomas Point Shoals Lighthouse – Chesapeake Bay, Maryland

Floating ice has always been a threat to screw-pile lighthouses such as the Thomas Point Shoals Lighthouse, whose foundation was damaged by heavy ice floes in the winter of 1877. The impact of the ice overturned the Fresnel lens, damaging it so badly the lens had to be replaced. Over the years, tons of riprap have been placed around the piles to protect the lighthouse from further damage. The Thomas Point Lighthouse is the only unaltered screw-pile lighthouse in the United States that is still attached to its original foundation.

A Lighthouse Keeper – An Ordinary Hero

Cape Elizabeth, Maine, photo courtesy of The Lighthouse People

January 28, 1885

Marcus Hanna, principal keeper at Cape Elizabeth Light, Portland, Maine, couldn't wait until morning when his assistant keeper arrived for his shift. A terrible blizzard had hit during the night, one of the "coldest and most violent storms of snow, wind and vapor … that I have ever witnessed." All night Marcus sounded the steam fog whistle, despite being very sick and exhausted.

When the assistant arrived, Marcus climbed down the stairs and stepped outside into the freezing cold. Snow drifts were so thick, he had to crawl to the keeper's house, where he promptly fell asleep. At sunrise, his wife looked out the window and spotted a schooner stuck on a rocky ledge below the fog signal house.

She awakened Marcus, who struggled out of bed and back through the snow to alert the assistant keeper who had not seen the vessel. Together, they rushed to the edge of the water. Two half-frozen sailors hung from the rigging trying to escape the icy waves.

Hanna tried several times to toss a rope with a weighted end onto the ship. After failing to succeed, the assistant keeper retreated to the protection of the fog house. But despite the freezing temperatures, Hanna waded waist-deep into the water and tossed the line again, this time hitting his target. One of the sailors managed to get the line and tie it around himself, then Hanna pulled him to shore. Hanna threw the rope several more times before landing it on the ship where the other crewman was able to reach the line and tie it around his waist. His strength was failing as Hanna strained to pull the man to safety.

Just in time, the assistant keeper returned, and neighbors arrived to help haul the sailor to shore where dry clothes, hot food and drink awaited. Amazingly, Marcus Hanna recuperated from the ordeal as well.

Six months later, he received a lifesaving medal for "heroism involving great peril to his life."

Marcus was a hero for his efforts. When asked later how he managed to prevail against the circumstances, he said, "I felt a terrible responsibility thrust upon me, and I resolved to attempt the rescue at any hazard."

Being a hero was the last thing on his mind when Marcus crawled into bed after putting in his time at the lighthouse that night. Sick, tired, and cold, all he wanted to do was rest. But when someone else's life was in danger, he put the needs of others before his own.

A hero is "one who performs courageous acts." Courage is "the quality of mind or spirit that enables a person to face difficulty, danger, or pain without fear."

Most of us aren't called to perform acts of courage like Marcus. But we still face challenges at times requiring us to step outside of our comfort levels. Even if we struggle with fear and doubt, we can trust God to be with us. In the Bible, He tells us to take courage. How? By knowing He is with us and will give us the courage we need.

"Be strong and courageous. Do not be afraid; do not be discouraged, for the Lord your God will be with you wherever you go." Joshua 1:9

Reflections

What challenges do you need God's courage to face? Will you focus on the challenge or the fact that God is with you?

Beacon Briefs

Cape Elizabeth, Maine, Lighthouse

Cape Elizabeth received its name from Captain John Smith in 1614, in honor of Princess Elizabeth, King Charles' sister. The first lighthouse built in 1811 was considered insufficient, considering the amount of marine traffic entering the Portland, Maine, harbor. In 1828, two towers were built, one with a fixed light and the other a revolving one, to distinguish them from other lighthouses in the area. These lighthouses were then referred to as "the twin lights of Cape Elizabeth."

Refuge in the Lighthouse

LaJument Lighthouse, photo by and courtesy of Jean Guichard

Perhaps the most famous lighthouse picture, the photo taken by French photographer Jean Guichard in 1989 has been featured on posters and calendars throughout the world.

The dramatic image of La Jument Lighthouse being engulfed by a monster wave is amazing and awe-inspiring. One can almost feel the tremendous power of the water as it surrounds the tower. A closer look reveals a man standing in the doorway. One's first reaction is to gasp and think this isn't a real picture, that it is trick photography, since a real person couldn't possibly survive such a situation.

However, the photograph is real and so is the man. For days, waves had pounded the structure during a fierce storm. Guichard had gone out in a helicopter to photograph the lighthouse during the tempest. What he didn't know at the time was that the two lighthouse keepers had been waiting to be rescued as waves shook the building and smashed windows.

Upon hearing the sound of Guichard's helicopter, Keeper Theodore Malgorn went outside to see if it was the rescue helicopter. When he realized it wasn't, he hurried back inside just as the wave was breaking over the lighthouse, avoiding certain death. The tower stood and the keepers survived.

In our own lives we face storms as well—emotional, financial, physical or others. But we also have a place of refuge knowing God will be there with us to protect and carry us through them.

"For you have been my refuge, a strong tower against the foe." Psalm 61:3

Reflections

What storms are you facing? Where is your place of refuge?

Beacon Briefs

La Jument Lighthouse, France

The La Jument area is heavily trafficked and experiences severe weather much of the year. Many shipwrecks occurred and lives lost over the centuries, stressing the need for a lighthouse. A wealthy Frenchman who almost died in one of these shipwrecks privately financed the construction of the lighthouse which began in 1904 but wasn't finished until 1911 due to the challenging conditions. Automated in 1991, its beacon still keeps watch today.

The Lighthouse Nobody Wanted

Little River Light, Cutler, Maine, photo courtesy of *Lighthouse Digest* magazine

I t's not the biggest, the prettiest, the oldest or the most important lighthouse. But to some people, it's the most valuable.

The Little River Lighthouse was first built in 1846 on an island in the Bay of Fundy, marking the entrance to the harbor at Cutler, Maine, the northernmost harbor on the US east coast. In 1876, the lighthouse was rebuilt and was an active aid to navigation until 1975.

After the station was automated, the Coast Guard left

the island, and the government attempted to maintain the station with caretakers for a short time before abandoning the station altogether. The house was boarded up and it, along with the lighthouse, was left to the elements. When the government planned to destroy the 1888 keeper's house, local citizens rose up and saved it from demolition. However, when the government offered the lighthouse to the town of Cutler in 1993, they declined, unable to handle the cost for restoration and maintenance of the tower and the house.

Next, the property was offered to the State of Maine, but they refused it as well.

So did the National Park Service when it was proposed to them.

The U.S. Fish & Wildlife Department responded in the same manner.

The future looked bleak for the lighthouse.

However, in 2000, the US Congress passed the National Historic Lighthouse Preservation Act, which allows nonprofits to apply for ownership of lighthouses.

In 2002, Little River Lighthouse became the first lighthouse in New England and the third lighthouse in the United States to have its ownership transferred to a nonprofit organization, the American Lighthouse Foundation.

Funds for the restoration were solicited from corporations, but most of the money and labor came from volunteers. Due to their efforts, the house was renovated, the light was relit, and the lighthouse became a model for lighthouse preservation, showing what can be accomplished when someone cares.

Can you identify with a lighthouse no one wanted it — outcast, abandoned, and rejected again and again? To most of the world, it was insignificant and unimportant. The situation seemed hopeless. And yet, a new future awaited, giving the lighthouse new value and purpose. In the same way, our lives can change from hopeless to meaningful if we trust God and wait for his timing.

"For I know the plans I have for you," declares the LORD, *"plans to prosper you and not to harm you, plans to give you hope and a future."* Jeremiah 29:11

Reflections

Do you feel hopeless, ready to give up? Turn to God, the god of hope who never gives up on us.

Beacon Briefs

Little River Lighthouse, Maine

In the late 1800's, Cutler, Maine, was a popular summer resort. Since fog often rolls in across the bay, steamships had to navigate the rocks around the island, relying on the light from the lighthouse and the fog signal. Even with their help, several steamers ran aground. The lighthouse keeper and his family provided food and shelter to the boats' passengers.

The General Who Built Lighthouses

Carysfort Reef, Florida, photo courtesy of The Lighthouse People

General George Meade is recognized as the Commander of the Union Army who won the Battle of Gettysburg, the turning point of the U.S. Civil War. His military judgment and tactical decisions proved his leadership abilities in challenging situations, including the second Seminole War and the Mexican American War.

Yet, before he was a military leader, George Meade, like many of his West Point classmates, was an engineer. In his career with the Army Corps of Topographical Engineers, Meade designed and constructed lighthouses in and around the Delaware Bay, New Jersey, and the Florida Keys.

Meade felt the United States was behind world standards in lighthouse construction. He first implemented a design previously used in England called the screwpile lighthouse when he built the lighthouse at Brandywine Shoal, Delaware.

After being sent to Florida, he adapted the screwpile construction technique to fight the effects of the Florida reefs and numerous hurricanes. Under his authority, the Carysfort Reef Lighthouse, the Sand Key Lighthouse, and the Sombrero Key Lighthouse were built.

Returning to New Jersey, Meade oversaw construction of the Barnegat Lighthouse, the Cape May Lighthouse, and the Rebecca Shoal Lighthouse. The Lighthouse Board was so impressed with his work that he was appointed guardianship over two lighthouse districts.

George Meade had a variety of names—general, commander, leader, engineer, and lighthouse builder.

Jesus was known by several names as well—Rabbi (teacher), Lord (God), Emmanuel (God with us), Christ (anointed one), Redeemer, Messiah (liberator), Savior (one who saves others from destruction) and others.

In the same way, we're all known by different names to different people—mother, father, daughter, son, husband, wife, teacher, pilot, businessman, etc.

There are names we like to be called, others we don't. One name I like to claim is believer in God.

"A good name is more desirable than great riches; to be esteemed is better than silver or gold." Proverbs 22:1

Reflections

By what names are you known? Of what name are you most proud?

Beacon Briefs

Carysfort Reef, Florida

Carysfort Reef Lighthouse, completed in 1852, is the oldest reef lighthouse off the coast of Florida and is named after one of its numerous reef victims, the HMS frigate Carysfort, which wrecked there in 1770.

Step By Step

Pensacola Lighthouse, Florida, photo courtesy of The Lighthouse People

peered up the endless spiral of stairs. In the pitch dark, I couldn't see how many more steps there were to the top. In fact, with my flashlight, I could only see one or two steps at a time. Hugging the wall of the old lighthouse, I ascended with no railing to keep me from falling into the abyss on the other side. Slowly, I made my way up, counting the steps.

But soon I lost track of how many steps I'd climbed of the 177 total, so I couldn't determine how much farther I had to go. Looking behind was pointless, as those steps had already disappeared into black shadows. I stopped at one of the two windows along the stairwell to catch my breath and gaze out. But it was a moonless sky, revealing nothing. Should I go back down or keep going up? If I was near the top, I might give up too soon and never meet my goal of reaching the summit.

Many years ago, lighthouse keepers ascended these same stairs at least twice a day to tend the light. The tallest lighthouse on the Gulf of Mexico, the Pensacola Lighthouse must have been a challenge to maintain, the keepers having to climb the steps while hauling a heavy bucket of oil and no flashlight. Instead, they balanced a lantern in one hand and the oil in the other.

Did they get tired and want to quit? It takes determination and dedication to the goal to keep going up those stairs. They believed their efforts made a difference. Who knows how many lives were saved because of their daily effort?

In much the same way, our lives are like going up those steps in the dark with only a small light for illumination. We can only see one or two steps at a time. So we keep moving toward the goal to reach the top, the end of the journey. Sometimes, we want to know more about what we'll encounter along the way or what the end result will be.

But God chooses not to give us too much information at once. We don't know our entire life's story, but He does. So we must live one day at a time, one step at a time. We have just enough light to keep from stumbling or falling off the edge. We can't go back to the beginning and start over, so we keep focusing on the step in front of us. Looking back doesn't help either; we must move forward to make progress. Each step is a step of faith and trust in an unknown future. Only God knows where we're headed, and He'll meet us at the end.

"A person's steps are directed by the Lord. How then can anyone understand their own way?" Proverbs 20:24

Reflections

How do you reach your goal if you can't see your way to the top? Are you trusting God to show you the next step to take?

Beacon Briefs

Pensacola Lighthouse, Florida

During the US Civil War, Confederate troops camped out at the base of the lighthouse which overlooks the entrance of Escambia Bay to the port of Pensacola, Florida. For a year, Union forces claiming Fort Pickens on Santa Rosa Island across the water exchanged fire with the Confederates at the lighthouse, with many shells hitting the building.

Unique Transportation to the Lighthouse

Tillamook Rock Lighthouse, Oregon, photo courtesy of The Lighthouse People

How do you get to work? Do you drive a car? Ride a bus? A train? A boat?

Or do you walk? Ride a bicycle? Motorcycle? What about a helicopter?

There are many different ways to get to places, but some lighthouse keepers had more challenging conditions to conquer before they could get to their jobs.

At places like Tillamook Rock Lighthouse in Oregon, Saddleback Ledge in Maine, and St. George Reef in California, a boatswain's (bosun's) chair was used to transport people from boats to the top of the island. A swinging crane erected on land connected by cable to the mast of a ship. Suspended from this cable was a board on

47

which a person sat as he or she was lifted up to travel between the ship and the island.

This type of transportation was not for the weak of heart, especially for those afraid of heights. Chances were also good that the person being transported would get wet, splashed by waves, if not dipped into the water.

Nubble Lighthouse in Maine and South Solitary Lighthouse in Australia used baskets to haul people and goods from ships to the lighthouse. Maneuvering these baskets required great skill to lift the occupants high enough to protect them from danger of being dropped onto rocky cliffs or into deep water.

When the phrase, "give someone a lift" was coined in 1712, it didn't refer to lighthouses in particular, but to offer them a ride, certainly appropriate for those who had to travel by bosun chair or basket. The word "lift" also refers to raising someone's spirits.

There are times when I need lifting up too. At those times, I turn to God, who can elevate my spirit and give me a "faith-lift."

"He lifted me out of the slimy pit, out of the mud and mire; he set my feet on a rock and gave me a firm place to stand. He put a new song in my mouth, a hymn of praise to our God." Psalm 40:2, 3

Reflections

Could you use a faith-lift today? Are your feet set on a firm place?

Beacon Briefs

Tillamook Rock, Oregon

Perched on sheer cliffs over twenty stories high, the lighthouse on Tillamook Rock off the coast of Oregon, was one of the least popular assignments for lightkeepers. "Terrible Tilly" as the rock was commonly known, was subject to extreme storms causing waves to shoot rocks crashing into the lighthouse, damaging the lantern room and flooding the keepers' quarters.

Buddy, The Lighthouse Dog

Mount Desert Rock, Maine, photo courtesy of Jeremy D'Entremont

Buddy took his job seriously. As watchdog for the lighthouse, his devotion and service were outstanding. When ships approached Mount Desert Rock Lighthouse, he greeted them with enthusiastic barking. Often, he'd dive into the water to welcome newcomers to the island.

One of Buddy's duties was dragging driftwood up from the rocky shore for the keeper's family to use as firewood. His other, very important duty was to guard the children while they played outdoors.

One day the keeper's five-year-old son played outside near the house while his mother did housework. Unknown to her, the child wandered away. Half an hour later Buddy bounded into the house barking and whining to get her attention. The woman assumed the wet dog had just retrieved more driftwood and ordered him out of the house. He returned moments later with the child's soaked and tattered hat, dropping it at her feet.

The alarmed mother ran from the house and followed Buddy, finding her child lying on the beach unconscious, wet and cold. He had apparently fallen into the sea and the dog had plunged in after him and dragged the child to safety. Though bruised and scratched, the child survived, thanks to Buddy's watchful eye and quick response.

The Coast Guard files contain numerous stories of dog mascots. The animals were valuable co-workers among the people they served, working at lighthouses and lifesaving stations, lightships, and tenders. "Man's best friend" was often man's best assistant.

*Based on a true story by Kirk Monroe published in *Scribner's Magazine* in 1896.

"A friend loves at all times." Proverbs 17:17a

Reflections

Do you need a friend who will always love you? Will you let Jesus be your friend?

Beacon Briefs

Mount Desert Rock, Maine

Mount Desert Rock, a small barren island twenty-six miles off the coast of Maine, is one of the most isolated lighthouses and the site of many shipwrecks and rescues. At its highest point, the island is only twenty feet above sea level and during storms, it can be entirely submerged by waves. Because no vegetation is on the island, fishermen used to bring dirt and seeds to the keepers' families so vegetables could be grown. The soil and seed were planted in crevices of the rocks making the island quite colorful during the summer months. But the next winter's storms would wash it all away again.

The Monk and the Lighthouse

Hook Head Light, Ireland, photo courtesy of *Lighthouse Digest* magazine

Dubhan was distressed by the sight of another body. The Welsh monk ran to the sailor lying on the beach in the morning sun and knelt beside the man, hoping to find a sign of life. It was not to be, though, for the rocks of the rocky peninsula, or "hook" of land, had claimed another victim.

Determined to save other mariners from a similar fate, Dubhan lit a fire in a huge iron basket each night and hung it over the edge of the cliff as a warning. The warning system he created around 450 A.D. was continued by other monks from the monastery he founded nearby until the twelfth century. The Norman army conquered the area, having been told to land either on the hook or on a nearby point called the "crook," hence the term "by hook or by crook." In 1172, the Normans constructed a tower on the spot.

The "Tower of Hook" with its open fire at the top was operated by monks until the 1500's when Henry VIII dissolved all the monasteries. After a hundred years of darkness, the lighthouse was renovated in 1667 and has been in service ever since making it the oldest operating lighthouse in Ireland and one of the oldest in the world.

Dubhan's actions are similar to God's guiding of the Israelites through the desert with "the cloud by day and with light from the fire all night." Psalm 78:14)

We all need guidance, especially in darkness, whether that darkness is physical, emotional, or spiritual. God provides light to guide us through the darkness and protect us from injury and death.

"For you have delivered me from death and my feet from stumbling, that I may walk before God in the light of life." Psalm 56:13

Reflections

Light can keep you from stumbling. Are you dealing with a darkness and need God's light?

Beacon Briefs

Hook Head Lighthouse, County Wexford, Ireland

At over 800 years old, this ancient beacon is an excellent example of medieval architecture. Its light is now operated by remote control from the Commissioners of Irish Lights.

He Dreamed of a Lighthouse

St. Simons Lighthouse, Georgia, photo courtesy of The Lighthouse People

Bangor, Massachusetts, 1793

Twenty-six-year-old James Gould gazed at the sketch of his lighthouse. Someday he would build it, but not here in Massachusetts. He would build it somewhere in the south, although he didn't know where.

Meanwhile, he stayed busy managing a sawmill

buying lumber and supervising production. In addition, he was asked by his employer to build his new home, so James rolled up the lighthouse sketch and put it aside.

Two years later, James traveled to Savannah, Georgia in his new role as timber surveyor for the U.S. Government to find the best live oak to build ships for the first US Navy. He took his lighthouse plans with him, but the lighthouse would not be built yet, as he spent the next few years living in swampy areas among hostile Indians while doing his job.

In 1807, when the US Treasury advertised for a builder to construct a lighthouse on St. Simons Island, James jumped at the chance. However, he disagreed with the department's specifications. He submitted his proposal anyway with suggested changes and got the contract.

After four long years of labor, the lighthouse was finally ready to be lit in 1811. In addition, James was offered the position as the lighthouse keeper, a position he held for the next 27 years.

Although it took years before James saw his dream come true, he never gave up hope and continued to work toward his goal.

Sometimes, it seems we will never see our dreams become reality – that they're too hard to achieve with too many obstacles in the way. But we never know when the opportunity will arise for our dreams to come true, so we must not give up.

"May he give you the desire of your heart and make all your plans succeed." Psalm 20:4

Reflections

Do you have a dream? Ask God to help you fulfill it.

Beacon Briefs

St. Simons Light, Georgia

When Union soldiers invaded St. Simons in 1862, the retreating Confederate soldiers destroyed the original Gould lighthouse so their enemy couldn't use it. A second lighthouse of brick construction was built in 1872 and is still an active aid to navigation.

Safe Harbor

Great Stirrup Cay Light, Bahamas, photo by Carolyn Hess, courtesy of *Lighthouse Digest* magazine

May 1863

Willie Potts knew he'd landed one of the most desirable jobs in the Bahamas. Although he had been a keeper at other, older lighthouses in the islands, this new lighthouse built by Britain's Imperial Lighthouse Service was much easier to maintain.

The shortest tower in the Service at 75 feet, it had half

as many steps as the one at Great Isaac Cay. For an older keeper like Willie, this situation had a great advantage and was far less arduous. Standing at the base of the gleaming white building and gazing up, Willie was proud and honored to be its first keeper.

Great Stirrup's Cay was an isolated location, with no other inhabitants besides Willie and his wife. Calm and peaceful, the island was surrounded by turquoise water with a natural harbor that was one of the most protected areas for ships lying anchor. It wasn't uncommon to see British ships in the harbor, but soon he noticed other ships – either flying the Stars and Stripes of the United States or the Confederate flag of the southern American states.

Remaining neutral during the American Civil War, Britain still relied on cotton the Southern states exported. So throughout the war, Confederate blockade runners carried cotton to Nassau in the Bahamas and exchanged it for goods from England. Willie often watched with anxiety as Union ships hid out nearby, waiting to intercept the Confederates en route. More than once, he saw a chase take place from his perch in the lantern room, hearing guns firing as the Union Navy took pursuit.

Willie hoped and prayed no stray shots landed nearby. Who would have thought someone else's war would threaten his peace, and that his safe harbor would no longer be safe? It would be two more years until the Civil War ended, and peace returned to the island.

"In peace I will lie down and sleep, for you alone, Lord, make me dwell in safety." Psalm 4:8

Reflections

Everyone needs a place of peace and safety, a safe harbor. Where is yours?

Beacon Briefs

Great Stirrup Cay Lighthouse, Bahamas

The island of Great Stirrup Cay is now privately owned by a cruise line. Once manned by light keepers, the beautifully designed colonial lighthouse is now solar powered.

Reflections

Reflections: a mirror-like place of quiet and solitude — the broken Whole of life.

— Brenton Davis

Great Surrender: Innocence Reborn

...

The Wrong Light

Assategue Lighthouse, Virginia, photo courtesy of The Lighthouse People

October 1891

The USS Despatch, a 730-ton steamship powered its way from New York to Washington, D.C. to pick up President Benjamin Harrison and Secretary of the Navy Benjamin Tracy.

Built in 1873, the sleek steamship had undergone many changes in its lifetime of escorting convoys and delivering high government officials to ports all over the world. In 1880, the ship was transformed into the first presidential yacht, serving five different presidents over time, carrying them to inspections and ceremonial duties.

But as the Despatch traveled down the coastline of Virginia the night of October 10, 1891, it encountered a storm. When the ship's crew saw the light from the Assateague Lighthouse in Virginia, mistaking it for one from a lightship farther south and steered the ship off course and into shallow water. As a result, the ship grounded off Assateague Island where the waves battered it beyond repair.

Thanks to a lifesaving station nearby, the crew was rescued, but the ship was a total loss. All because of an error in judgment, a decision to change course to follow the wrong light ended in destruction.

Many have offered reasons why such a mistake could be made, especially since the ship had traveled the same route before. The storm, lack of visibility, or confusion could have been causes. However, the people in charge of the ship should have known their location by navigational tools and shouldn't have altered the course that had been set.

We as individuals often make similar mistakes. We know the way we should go, but we get lured off course by things that seem to be good options, then turn out to be poor ones. The key is to know our destination and the right way to get there and follow God's leading to make the right choices along the way.

"There are those who rebel against the light, who do not know its ways or stay in its paths." Job 24:13

Reflections

Have you veered off path? Pray for God to lead you back to the right one.

Beacon Briefs

Assateague Lighthouse, Virginia

From the top of the lighthouse, you can see herds of wild horses that live on the island. Horses have roamed the island over 300 years. Some claim they originally arrived as survivors of a shipwreck. Another possibility for their location is that early settles put their livestock on the island, perhaps to avoid fencing laws and taxes on livestock.

MARILYN TURK

A Stronger Lighthouse

Smeaton's Tower, England, photo by Dr. Karl Agre

The Eddystone Rocks are a treacherous reef off the southwest coast of England. Because the reef is submerged during high tides, it has been the site of many shipwrecks throughout history.

In 1698, the first lighthouse was built on the rocks, only to fall victim to the raging sea four years later. It was another five years before a new lighthouse, built in the same place, was lit. This lighthouse lasted until the lantern room caught fire, burning the structure to the ground.

In 1759, John Smeaton, a civil engineer, was hired to build a new lighthouse. Smeaton modeled his lighthouse in the shape of an oak tree, with the base being larger than the top, the first lighthouse to be designed in this manner. He also pioneered the technique of securing granite blocks using dovetail joints and marble dowels. In addition, he

71

developed the use of hydraulic lime, a concrete that sets under water. As a result of these innovations, Smeaton's lighthouse outlasted its predecessors.

A hundred years later, erosion of rock under the tower plus the need for a larger building to house the latest lighting equipment required a new lighthouse. In 1884, after the new tower was built alongside the old one, the nearby city of Plymouth had the old Smeaton lighthouse taken down and rebuilt on city property as a memorial. The foundation, however, proved too difficult to dismantle, so the "stump" remained on the reef.

Smeaton's lighthouse was sturdier due to his engineering ability. But perhaps another clue to its longevity can be found in the lighthouse oil room. Still visible to those who visit the lighthouse at Plymouth today is an original inscription which encircles the top of the room. The words, "Except the Lord builds the house, they labor in vain who build it," a quote from Psalm 127. Perhaps Smeaton's faith was as important to his success as was the solid foundation of his lighthouse.

"He will be the sure foundation for your times, a rich store of salvation and wisdom and knowledge; the fear of the LORD is the key to this treasure." Isaiah 33:6

Reflections

Whose foundation are you building on? Is it as reliable as God's?

Beacon Briefs

A Stronger Lighthouse – Smeaton Tower, UK

John Smeaton was the first self-proclaimed "civil engineer," and is often called the "father of civil engineering." In addition to the lighthouse, he built bridges, canals, and harbors.

The Lighthouse and the Judas Lantern

Monomoy Point Light, Massachusetts, photo courtesy of Jeremy D'Entremont

S hipwreck!"

The word brought alarm to some, prosperity to others. In the days of sailing and few lighthouses, shore-side residents often saw the event as a source of unexpected treasure.

Once the survivors were taken to shore, the motto "finders, keepers" was the rule for anything left on the ship or washed up on the shore. In the poor villages of Key West, the Bahamas, North Carolina's Outer Banks, or England's Cornish Coast, the event was hailed as a sign of divine providence. Often these people prayed for a shipwreck and thanked God for the bounty it would provide. Everything from crates of fruit to furniture and exotic goods were discovered among the salvage of these ships.

Of course in areas where shipwrecks were more common, the unscrupulous turned to "mooncussing," a practice of using false lights, called "Judas Lanterns," to intentionally lure ships onto rocks in order to profit from the salvage. Since bright moonlit nights rendered the false lights ineffective, the criminals would curse the moon.

The procedure for mooncussing involved a lantern, a rope and a horse. The lamp was tied to hang below the horse's neck and the rope was tied to one of its legs. When the mooncusser pulled the roped horse up and down the beach, the uneven gait made the lantern swing similar to a ship's lantern when the vessel is anchored. As ships steered toward the false lights thinking the area was safe, they ended up wrecking on rocks or sandbars.

Legend has it that Nags Head, North Carolina was named for a mooncusser's horse. Other tales of mooncussers recounted by sailors from Australia to Cape Cod warned of areas where the practice was known to exist. Eventually, lighthouses were built in these areas to warn ships of the dangers in those areas. The reliable light of the lighthouses saved ships, but the Judas lights were their doom.

"The Lord is my light and my salvation— whom shall I fear?" Psalm 27:1

Reflections

Are you following the true light that saves or the false light that leads to disaster?

Beacon Briefs

Monomoy Point Light, Massachusetts

When Monomoy Point Light was built, it was on a peninsula, but erosion and shifting sands changed the peninsula to an island. Deactivated in 1923, most of the guests to the lighthouse now are the winged kind, with ten species of native birds and over 285 species of migratory birds visiting each year.

The Socialite Lighthouse Keeper

Point Pinos Light, California, courtesy of The Lighthouse People

Emily Fish stared out the window of her elegant home in San Francisco, watching Que, her Chinese gardener, work in her manicured lawn. She exhaled a huge sigh and turned from the window where her eyes focused on valuable artwork on the walls, antique furnishings, and the table set with fine china. She had everything anyone could want, but there was a huge void in her heart since her husband's death. What would she do now?

At dinner, her daughter Juliet and her husband, Lt. Cmdr. Henry Nichols, a Navy officer and lighthouse inspector, tried to console her.

"Mother, you need to get out and visit. Have tea with

your friends," Juliet pleaded.

"Juliet, after 33 years as a housewife, I want to do something useful."

Henry cleared his throat, hoping to change the subject.

"Allen Luce is retiring from Point Pinos. Been the keeper there for 22 years. His resignation sort of took us by surprise and we don't know who will take over his position yet."

Emily straightened in her chair. "I want to do it. I want to be the lighthouse keeper at Point Pinos."

"But Mother, you've never done anything like that! And you'll be away from your friends," her daughter argued.

"I want to be of service to others. As a doctor, your father spent his life helping people. I'm not a physician, but I can tend a light to help those at sea. Besides, Point Pinos isn't as remote as other lighthouses, being close to Monterey."

"But most women became keepers to take the place of their keeper husbands who died, as they were already familiar with the duties," Henry said. "Plus, there's a lot of physical work."

"Que will go with me. Between the two of us, we can do the job."

Persuaded, Henry put in for Emily's appointment and in 1893, she and Que packed up their furnishings and moved into the modest lighthouse at Point Pinos, Emily transformed the little house into a stylish cottage, had topsoil delivered to the expansive lighthouse property, and planted trees, grass, and a cypress hedge. She also brought in thoroughbred horses, Holstein cows, and white leghorn chickens.

Emily began hosting small dinner parties, giving her the nickname of the "socialite lightkeeper." But keeping an elegant house, a manicured lawn, and socializing was not Emily's main focus. She threw herself into her job, determined to perform her duties well. As a lightkeeper, she kept meticulous logs and a spotless lighthouse. Her standards were high, in fact, too high for the thirty male assistants she hired and fired during her twenty-year career, calling them incompetent. Lighthouse inspectors always found the station in excellent condition and commended her for a job well done.

Emily Fish found a new purpose in life when she devoted herself to serving others. Her gifts of hospitality, organization, and efficiency proved useful for her position as lighthouse keeper.

"Each of you should use whatever gift you have received to serve others as faithful stewards of God's grace in its various forms." 1 Peter 4:10

Reflections

What gifts has God given you that can benefit others?

Beacon Briefs

Point Pinos Lighthouse, California

Charles Layton was the first keeper of the light when it was activated in 1855, with his wife Charlotte as his assistant. While riding in a posse pursuing bandit Anastacio Garcia, Keeper Layton was shot and later died of his wounds, leaving Charlotte in charge of the lighthouse until her second husband became keeper five years later.

Sunrise at the Lighthouse

West Quoddy Light, Maine, courtesy of The Lighthouse People

Where on earth does the sun rise first? For the continental United States, that distinction belongs to the West Quoddy Head Lighthouse at Lubec, Maine. Located on the easternmost point of the country, the site is the first place to experience the splendor of the rising sun.

Imagine standing outside the tower as the sky slowly changes from black to lavender-gray, then becomes streaked with pink, orange and gold which outline the clouds above the horizon as the glowing orb emerges. Visualize the ocean below as it reflects the mirror image of the changing sky above with colors that tinge the water in vibrant hues.

Soon the haze of dawn begins to clear, the horizon divides the heavens above from the sea, and objects emerge with clarity. The sky boasts tones of blue as the sun breaks through the clouds and declares itself ruler of the day.

Malcom Rouse, last Coast Guard keeper at the West Quoddy Head Lighthouse once remarked, "I'm up when that sunshine hits here—it's the first place it hits—it sure is beautiful."

So do the people on the west coast of the United States feel disappointed because they're the last ones to see the sun rise? Not at all, because the daily miracle of a sunrise can be witnessed from any place on the earth. Wherever they are, people have the opportunity to watch the sun come up as the earth rotates on its axis. Everyone has the chance to witness the beginning of a new day.

"The steadfast love of the LORD never ceases, his mercies never come to an end; they are new every morning; great is your faithfulness." Lamentations 3:22-23 NRSV

Reflections

Isn't it encouraging to know that each day is a new beginning and a chance to start over?

Beacon Briefs

West Quoddy, Maine

Legend has it that fog is manufactured in the Bay of Fundy where the West Quoddy Lighthouse sits at the juncture to Passamaquoddy Bay. In 1826, Congress passed an act to pay the keeper at West Quoddy extra salary for the time he spent ringing the fog bell.

Sending the Wrong Message

Fort Point, Maine, courtesy of The Lighthouse People

"Ernie, I'll put up the flag this morning, since you have so much to do," Polly said to her husband Ernie DeRaps, the lightkeeper at Fort Point Lighthouse in Maine.

"Thanks." Ernie said on his way out the door.

Every morning Ernie started the day by raising the American flag and saluting it. Sometimes Polly helped with those duties as well.

She hadn't realized the wind was so strong that cold morning when she volunteered to raise it by herself, struggling to get the flag attached to the rope while a gusty wind wrapped the cloth around her. Finally, she succeeded in pulling the flag to the top of the flagpole, tied the rope around the cleat to secure it, and rushed inside to get out of the cold. She didn't look back as she began her household chores.

There wasn't any boat traffic that frosty winter day until later in the afternoon when she saw a small tanker make its way into the bay. About that time, the phone rang. Polly answered it and a gruff voice asked, "What's your problem?"

"Why, there's nothing wrong here," Polly stated, confused about the question.

"Well, this is the Coast Guard base at Rockland, and you have a distress signal flying. We have a Coast Guard cutter, and another boat headed your way, as well as a plane coming from Salem." Polly's face grew hot as the stern caller continued to list all the emergency vehicles coming to her rescue. What should she do? She and Ernie were very conscientious with the duties at the lighthouse. Was her husband in trouble?

The caller paused and the phone went silent. Then the voice softened. "Polly, is the flag flying upside down? Go outside and check it. You know that's a sign of distress. By the way, nothing is on its way to your place. I was just kidding, but don't let it happen again."

Polly breathed a sigh of relief, then recognized the caller, a friend. Torn between being angry for scaring her and thankful he wasn't serious, she hurried out to correct her mistake. From then on, no matter the weather, she made sure she looked up each time she put out the flag to make sure it was flying properly.

Sometimes we make mistakes in communication. We mean one thing but someone else understands another. Or we say something we wish we could take back. But when we do, we can try to fix them, apologize, or correct the error and hope our mistake will be forgiven.

Thank God, He forgives us when we've said or done the wrong thing and gives us another chance to get it right.

"Indeed, there is no one on earth who is righteous, no one who does what is right and never sins."
Ecclesiastes 7:20

Reflections

Are you carrying around guilt for making a mistake?
Confess it to God and he'll help you carry the burden.

Beacon Briefs

Fort Point Lighthouse, Maine

Fort Point Lighthouse, established in 1856, was named
for the British fort built nearby in 1759 as a protection
against the French and Native Americans.

The Lady Who Was a Lighthouse

Statue of Liberty, New York, photo courtesy of The Lighthouse People

A lthough the lady is over one hundred years old, she stands tall and proud at the entrance to New York's Harbor.

Famous for her imposing stature and regal form, the Statue of Liberty has represented freedom to thousands of immigrants. The people of France named her "Libertas," after the Roman goddess for freedom, when they built her and shipped her over as a gift to the United States.

In her right hand, she holds a torch representing enlightenment or progress and in her left, she holds a tablet inscribed with the date of America's Declaration of Independence, July 4, 1776. Since her establishment on the island leading into the harbor, thousands of ships have hailed her as their welcome to the country.

She retains another unique position in that she was a lighthouse governed by the US Lighthouse Board from 1886 to 1901 and owns the distinction of being the first lighthouse lit by electricity. Her torch, held 305 feet in the air, contained nine electric arc lamps and could be seen 24 miles out to sea. In fact, the first lightkeeper, Albert Littlefield, received a higher salary than any other lightkeeper because he was familiar with the "new" technology.

Although the torch was extinguished many years ago and her status as a lighthouse removed, flood lighting was installed to reveal the entire figure at night. Therefore, now her whole body reflects light for all to see.

On the Fourth of July, she is emblazoned by thousands of fireworks set off in the harbor as the United States celebrates its freedom, commemorating the words at her base: *""Give me your tired, your poor, your huddled masses yearning to breathe free. The wretched refuse of you teaming shore. Send these, the homeless, tempest-tossed to me, I lift my lamp beside the golden door!"*

Yet there is another who offers safe haven and eternal freedom. Thank God for setting us free from a life that has entangled us in despair and shame. Christ's offer of sanctuary is permanent.

"Come to me, all you who are weary and burdened, and I will give you rest." Matt. 11:28

Reflections

What would you like to be free from? Are there bad habits, guilt or shame that hold you captive?

Beacon Briefs

The Statue of Liberty, New York

French sculptor of "Lady Liberty", Frederic Auguste Bartholdi, was inspired by ancient statues and supposedly modeled her after the Colossus of Rhodes.

How to Hide a Lighthouse

Cape Canaveral Light, Florida, photo courtesy of The Lighthouse People

Hide a lighthouse? Sounds impossible, doesn't it? One way would be to turn off the lights.

That's exactly what happened in the Civil War.

In July 1861, in an effort to hinder the Union Navy, the Confederate Treasury ordered all Southern lighthouses keepers to extinguish their lights.

But many Confederate soldiers and sympathizers took the order even farther. They dismantled the expensive and delicate lenses of many lighthouses and packed them into crates to keep the lights from falling into enemy hands. Many were shipped to other locations for hiding. When Union General Sherman captured the North Carolina courthouse, he found numerous lenses hidden there. Other lighthouse lenses were hidden in more obscure or creative locations.

Keeper Mills Burnham of the Cape Canaveral, Florida, lighthouse dismantled his lantern and packed the prisms in crates, then buried them in his orange grove where they remained until after the war.

Confederate soldiers buried the parts of the Port Aransas, Texas, lighthouse in a nearby marsh, but the location was lost, and the lantern was never found. At Matagorda Island, Texas, the lighthouse lantern was buried in the sand. This lantern, too, was never found later.

Another lighthouse lantern was buried in a cemetery with its own headstone, and the lantern parts of Florida's Jupiter Light were found in a nearby creek.

The Union government had quite a challenge finding all the hidden lighthouse lenses after the war when they began to put the lighthouses back into service. Some were never found and had to be remade. Others had to be repaired. It took several years, but eventually the lighthouses were relit and restored, once again functioning as navigational aids.

"Search me, God, and know my heart; test me and know my anxious thoughts. See if there is any offensive

way in me and lead me in the way everlasting. " Psalm 139:23-24

Reflections

Is there anything you're trying to hide? Uncover it and ask the Lord to remove it from you.

Beacon Briefs

Cape Canaveral Lighthouse, Florida

Cape Canaveral's first keeper left his position at the 1848 lighthouse after threats of attack by Seminole Indians.

Supernatural Strength

Old postcard of Lime Rock Light, courtesy of Jeremy D'Entremont

Hosea Lewis watched in fear as Ida, his sixteen-year-old daughter, rowed the heavy wooden boat bearing her three younger siblings through rough waves, afraid the next wave would capsize the boat. From his wheelchair, he could only observe the scene from the lighthouse window, helpless to offer any assistance. Yet, somehow, Ida managed to safely transport the children back and forth from Lime Rock Island to school in Newport, Rhode Island, on the mainland every day.

Soon after becoming the lighthouse keeper of the Lime Rock light station in 1853, Mr. Lewis had suffered a stroke, and responsibilities for the lighthouse fell to his wife and his oldest child, Ida.

Ida became famous for her skill and strength, unusual for a young woman. Her first rescue was in 1858 when she rowed out to rescue four boys whose small sailboat had capsized. In another incident, she rescued two soldiers as they clung to their overturned boat.

Soon, reports of Ida's heroic efforts and rescues of at least eighteen people from drowning reached the newspapers.

Ida eventually became the official lighthouse keeper, serving in the position from 1879 to 1911. Her last recorded rescue happened when she was 63 years old. When she was interviewed later in life and asked where she found her strength and courage, she said, "I don't know, I ain't particularly strong. The Lord Almighty gives it to me when I need it, that's all."

"It is God who arms me with strength and keeps my way secure." 2 Samuel 22:33

Reflections

Could you use some extra strength?

Beacon Briefs

Lime Rock Light, Rhode Island

Lime Rock Light was renamed Ida Lewis Light and is now the clubhouse of the Ida Lewis Yacht Club.

A New Beginning

Morris Island Light, South Carolina, photo courtesy of The Lighthouse People

’ve been here a long time, over 200 years so far. I remember when I was brand-new, before the American Civil War. I’ve watched all types of boats pass by, showing them the right way to go, and warning them where not to go. A lot has changed since I was young, yet I’ve survived.

It was harrowing to be on my island in the middle of

the entrance to Charleston harbor during the Civil War. Both sides wanted my service. I only wanted to perform the duty for which I was built, yet I was damaged, taken apart, even partially destroyed. It was a relief when the war ended and they rebuilt me, gave me new lens, new paint, and renewed my life. Yet, after my rebuilding, they altered the channels, and the changed course caused the sea to beat mercilessly against my island, stealing bits of it and reducing its size. But the sea left me alone—for a while.

Then in 1885, a hurricane attacked the Atlantic coast, destroying many of the buildings and bridges around me. My light was out for a few days, but soon I was shining again after they repaired my damage. For another year.

However, in 1886, a severe earthquake rocked our area, knocking out my lens and cracking my tower. But once more, I was repaired and survived to shine again.

For another hundred years, I manned my position, while erosion removed more of my island. I watched them build another lighthouse on the northern side of the harbor, assuming, I guess, that I might not survive much more erosion. But I did, and then another, bigger problem occurred.

In 1989, Hurricane Hugo hit our coast with such ferocity that it wiped out all the remaining buildings on my island. Where once there were fifteen, including a keeper's house, a little schoolhouse, and others, now there was nothing else but me. I stood alone. The government decided my light was no longer needed and started using the newer one on the other side instead.

Now, I have no island and no light. I stand alone in the water. But there are people who still care about me, and they started a group to help me. They've built a new barrier around me to help me stand, and they're planning to make me a famous tourist attraction. Me! Famous! After all these years of wars, hurricanes, earthquakes, and erosion, I still stand.

"We are hard pressed on every side, but not crushed; perplexed, but not in despair; persecuted, but not abandoned; struck down, but not destroyed." 2 Corinthians 4:8-9

Reflections

Do you sometimes feel like you're pressed on every side like the Morris Island Lighthouse? Take heart because God has not abandoned you and He will help you stand.

Beacon Briefs

A New Beginning - Morris Island Light, South Carolina

The first lighthouse on Morris Island was ordered by King Charles III of England and built in 1767. Ongoing efforts continue to preserve and restore the battered lighthouse.

Peace in the Storm

Great Point (Nantucket) Light, Massachusetts, photo courtesy of The
Lighthouse People

William Smith was anxious to show off his splendid schooner to his new bride Olivia. But Olivia was afraid of the water after hearing tales of shipwrecks and drownings. Even when she married her dashing sea captain, she never intended to join him on a boat.

"Olivia, darling, there's nothing to be afraid of. I've made this day trip scores of times, and my crew is quite experienced. I promise we'll be back home safely in Cape Cod by dusk."

Olivia's hand trembled as she accepted his. "All right. But you must keep your promise."

Looking at his lovely new bride, William wanted to prove he could take care of her. "I promise."

But as the shoreline diminished behind them, the

clouds grew darker, and the wind picked up. Soon the waves were pitching the boat up and down, splashing its passengers with icy cold water. The crew frantically tried to steady the boat and turn it back to shore, but the wind was too strong, carrying them farther out.

William clutched his wife and helped her to the small cabin. "Stay in here where you'll be safe."

Terror gripped her heart as Olivia watched her husband go back to the deck. Never had she felt so helpless. Trying to steady herself inside the cabin, all she could do was pray.

Dear Lord, please protect us and bring us safely to shore.

Shouts came from the men outside. "There's a light! We're heading toward the lighthouse!

The lighthouse! They were near the shore. But her glimmer of hope disappeared when the boat shuddered to a crashing stop. Slamming onto rocks, it cracked and splintered and began to break apart.

William ran inside, grabbed Olivia, and leaped into the chilly water with her in his arms. Holding her tightly, he swam toward the lighthouse; his crew jumping in behind.

As they climbed onto the rocks, they were met by Great Point Lighthouse keeper George Swain and his wife who helped them inside their home. The grateful shipwreck victims warmed themselves by the fire, resting from the turmoil of the storm. Olivia closed her eyes as she absorbed the peace and quiet, thankful her prayer had been answered.

"You will keep in perfect peace those whose minds are steadfast, because they trust in you." Isaiah 26:3

Reflections

Do you need peace in the storms of life?

Beacon Briefs

Great Point Light, Massachusetts

Also known as the Nantucket Light, the original stone Great Point Lighthouse, built in 1817, was destroyed by a storm in 1983 and rebuilt in 1986.

An Unexpected Guest at the Lighthouse

New Dungeness Light, Washington, photo by Ron Foster, courtesy of
Lighthouse Digest magazine

New Dungeness Lighthouse, Washington, 1868

The whooping of a tribe of Native Americans had awakened Lighthouse Keeper Henry Blake and his wife Mary Ann during the night. It wasn't unusual to see the peaceful natives camping on the beach on their way to or from British Colombia, but these sounds were unnerving.

Keeper Blake grabbed his gun and opened the door a crack. A moan caused him to look down where a Native woman lay bleeding, her arm reaching out for help.

He called his wife to help carry the young woman inside. She was pregnant and had been stabbed multiple times. The keeper and his wife washed and bandaged the woman's wounds, then gave her some warm tea to stop her shivering.

In broken English, the woman told them her band of Indians had been attacked while they slept. Everyone in her party had been killed except her, who pretended to be dead until the raiders left, taking everything they could from the bodies. Somehow, she had crawled to the lighthouse keeper's house for aid.

Keeper Blake went up to the tower to look. Bodies lay motionless near the campsite.

When he returned downstairs, there was a knock at the door. Taking his gun, he opened the door to find several members of an enemy tribe. Blake aimed his gun at them.

"Go away from here," he said.

"Give us woman!" they demanded.

"No! And if you come any closer, I'll shoot."

"Give us woman!"

Blake stepped forward, aiming the gun at them. "Go! Now!"

The Natives looked at each other, then left.

The Blakes made sure the woman had food and a safe, warm place to stay before her wounds healed and she returned to her own people.

Twenty Years Later
New Dungeness Lighthouse

Keeper Edward Brooks greeted the young Native American brave who landed in a dugout canoe near the lighthouse.

"You the lighthouse keeper?" the man said.

"Yes, I am. What can I do for you?"

"I come to say thank you for saving my life." He extended his hand.

"I'm sorry, but I don't remember meeting you."

"You saved my mother when she carried me."

"Come inside. I'd like to hear your story." Brooks invited him to join them for dinner.

Keeper Brooks had heard about the Indian massacre that occurred near the lighthouse when Henry Blake was the keeper. Now it was his turn to extend hospitality.

"Do not forget to show hospitality to strangers, for by so doing some people have shown hospitality to angels without knowing it." Hebrews 13:2 NIV

Reflections

Who can you show hospitality to today?

Beacon Briefs

New Dungeness Lighthouse, Washington

Established in 1857. and still an active aid to navigation, New Dungeness was the last lighthouse on the West Coast manned by the Coast Guard. The final keeper left in 1994.

Ice Castles and Frozen Lighthouses

Racine Reef Light, Wisconsin, photo courtesy of Terry Pepper

Winter's storms can change the appearances of lighthouses into surreal works of art. Perhaps the most photographed are the lighthouses of the Great Lakes, which become beautiful ice castles when stormy waves meet freezing temperatures. These awe-inspiring pictures lead one to wonder if anyone was ever inside the lighthouses and what they would experience.

On the Great Lakes, there is an open season of navigation which runs from around April to the end of December, when the lakes freeze over. Without shipping, there was no need for the lights or resident lightkeepers during that time. However, even before shipping shut down, there were often icy storms during which the lighthouse keepers had to maintain the lights. Although some of the lights were at the end of breakwaters and the keepers lived onshore, they had to walk over iced-over catwalks and piers to reach the lights.

In fact, there have been some lighthouse keepers who became stranded in their frozen lighthouses. One of these was the Racine Reef Lighthouse.

Located two and a half miles from the shore of Racine, Wisconsin, the lovely Victorian lighthouse whose architecture reflected that of the town, was built in 1906 to warn mariners traveling between Milwaukee and Chicago of the dangerous Racine Reef.

Several times in its history, the Racine Reef Lighthouse was encased in ice during December, preventing the lightkeepers from getting out and obtaining food and supplies. Once in 1929, the doors and windows were frozen shut, so without any chance of thawing, the men broke a window and chopped through the ice to escape. Another time, five Coast Guardsmen chained themselves together and pushed a skiff loaded with food three miles across the ice to reach the starving keepers.

Little wonder maritime traffic halts on the Great Lakes during the cold, icy winter.

Winter has the same effect on vegetation, forcing it to rest until spring's new growth begins. Much of the animal kingdom goes into hibernation during the winter as well.

Winter slows us down too, often closing airports, schools and businesses.

There's a reason for winter, and it's not just because the earth turns on its axis. God created seasons of the earth so the earth will function properly, with each season preparing the way for the next. In the same way, we have seasons in our lives. Whether it's a winter when we're resting and dormant, or a spring when life is abounding in blessings, each season has its own purpose and benefit. It may seem like winter has you "iced in" and unproductive. But remember, winter is a time of preparation for the next season of growth.

"There is a time for everything, and a season for every activity under the heavens." Ecclesiastes 3:1

Reflections

Are you going through a "winter" in your life? Expect springtime to come and ask God to show you how to prepare for it.

Beacon Briefs

Racine Reef Lighthouse, Wisconsin

In 1961 after the Racine Reef lighthouse was automated, the building was neglected. Unfortunately, the once picturesque lighthouse was torn down and replaced with a metal tower.

How Much is a Lighthouse Worth?

The Graves Light, Massachusetts, photo courtesy of The Lighthouse People

In 2013, The Graves Lighthouse sold for $933,888.00, the highest price ever paid for a lighthouse at government auction. Built in 1905, the stone tower stands on the outermost island of the Boston Harbor Islands and is only accessible by boat. The new owners began an extensive period of restoration to save the historic site. Why would someone pay so much for such a lighthouse, and one that still needs work? The new owners are antique collectors and believe saving a piece of history is worth the price.

Another man purchased his second lighthouse, the Manistique East Breakwater Lighthouse. Although the city of Manistique, Michigan could have acquired the lighthouse free of charge under the National Lighthouse Preservation Act, the city refused. So the government put the lighthouse up for auction to the highest bidder, and the lucky buyer won the bid for $15,000. Why did this man want the lighthouse when the city didn't? As a child growing up on Lake Erie, he developed a fondness for lighthouses, so for the second time in a year, having purchased the Liston Rear Range Lighthouse in Delaware for $22,000, he bought another one to save and preserve for future generations.

The 1899 Orient Point Lighthouse of New York was auctioned off for the second time and sold for $252,000. This lighthouse had once been considered so worthless, the Navy was going to blow it up in a demolition exercise. But huge public outcry prevented the destruction, so the Coast Guard spruced it up instead. And in 1999, a celebration was held to honor the lighthouse's 100 years of service.

It's interesting to note how a lighthouse can be considered worthless to some and valuable to others. What determines the value? The person willing to pay the price, whatever that price may be, because that person cares about the lighthouse and wants to save it.

In the same way, God cared so much about us that he placed the highest value on each of us. While we may seem worthless to others, God believes we have great value, so much so that he paid the highest price, his son, to save us.

"For God bought you with a high price" I Corinthians 6:20 (NLT)

Reflections

Do you sometimes feel worthless? Take heart knowing that God finds you valuable.

Beacon Briefs

Graves Lighthouse, Massachusetts

The Graves Lighthouse was not named for the number of shipwrecks in the area. It was named for Rear Admiral Thomas Graves, who pointed out the dangers of the area in 1634.

Too Much Trouble?

Elbow Reef Lighthouse, Bahamas, photo courtesy of Annie Potts

9 8, 99, 100!" - the keeper of the Elbow Reef Lighthouse trudged to the top of the staircase each night every two hours to wind the weights that turned the light.

Catching his breath, he looked out at the Bahamian waters. *You'd think these people would appreciate this light*, he thought. Before the lighthouse was built, at least one ship per month wrecked on the reef near Hope Town. In fact, the shipping companies lost so many ships, they appealed to the British government for help. The government responded by building the lighthouse in 1864.

The lighthouse saved the ships, but it put a major dent in the local economy. The business of "wracking," or scavenging shipwrecks, thrived in the area, and no shipwrecks meant no income. The hostilities had manifested themselves during the construction of the lighthouse when one of the lighthouse supply ships was sunk. Now the lightkeeper faced the same resentment in angry scowls and bitter remarks whenever he went to town.

The local opposition only added to the burden of his job, which the Imperial Light Service expected him to carry out efficiently. He still had to carry the kerosene to the top, trim the wicks, polish the brass, clean the windows, crank the mechanism, and keep the lighthouse spotless. *A lot of work with little reward.* But he continued to do his best to fulfill his duty day after day.

Each Imperial light station was furnished with signal flags to communicate with passing ships. The ships would use their own signal flags to identify themselves, share other news, or send requests for medical assistance. Sometimes, the ships and the lighthouses would simply make small talk via the flags.

One day as usual, the keeper noted a ship passing by, recording the name of the ship in his log. Then the ship proceeded to send another message. As the keeper recognized the words "Thank You," a broad smile crossed his face. He then hoisted his own flags to respond, "You're welcome." Somebody had finally acknowledged and appreciated his effort.

Often, we feel burdened by the responsibilities we face. Too many people with too many demands and little appreciation weigh us down. Yet, we don't have to carry the burden alone. God knows our challenges, and he has offered to help us carry the load.

"Come to me, all you who are weary and burdened, and I will give you rest." Matthew 11:28

Reflections

Are you weary and tired of carrying your burden? Let God give you rest.

Beacon Briefs

Elbow Reef, Bahamas

The Elbow Reef Lighthouse is the only remaining hand-wound kerosene-burning lighthouse in the world.

A Big Responsibility

New Canal Light, Louisiana, photo courtesy of The Lighthouse People

What was Madge going to do? Her husband, the keeper of the Head of Passes Light Station at the mouth of the Mississippi River in Louisiana, had just drowned, leaving her with two small children. What else, but take over her husband's duties? So in 1891, Margaret Norvell became a lighthouse keeper. In 1896, she was reassigned to be the keeper of the Port Pontchartrain Light Station on Lake Pontchartrain near New Orleans. And in 1924, Madge became lightkeeper for the New Canal Light, also in New Orleans, where she served until she retired in1932 at the age of 70. For 41years, she handled the job of keeper and was credited with rescuing many shipwrecked sailors. Once after receiving word that a Navy plane had crashed into the lake, she rowed two hours in a dangerous squall to rescue the pilot and return him to the lighthouse.

Madge became known as "the lady of the light." When she was interviewed after her retirement about her outstanding commitment, she replied, "There isn' anything unusual about a woman keeping a light in her window to guide people home. I just happen to keep a bigger light because I have so many people to get safely home." In other words, it was just her responsibility.

I wonder if she ever thought she couldn't handle the responsibility. Did she think the job was too big for her, too demanding? If she did, it didn't stop her from doing the best she could with what she had. Why? Because it was her duty to get people safely home.

Sometimes we're faced with responsibility which seems too big for us to handle. We doubt our ability and fear failure. Whatever our role—supervisor, employee, spouse, parent, grandparent, or caregiver—we wonder if we're up to the task. So how do we handle the responsibility?

The truth is, we don't have to handle it alone. God says He comes alongside us and helps us. We are not alone, and we don't have to rely on our ability. God can handle it. That's His job.

"Cast all your care upon Him, for He cares for you."
1 Peter 5:7

Reflections

Got a job too big to handle? You don't have to handle it alone.

Beacon Briefs

New Canal Light, Louisiana

In 2013, a US Coast Guard Sentinel class Fast Response cutter was named the "Margaret Norvell," the first cutter of its kind to be named for a woman. I was privileged to be invited for its commissioning in New Orleans, Louisiana, along with many of her descendants who were also on hand to honor her memory.

The Friendly Lighthouse

Cockspur Island Lighthouse, Georgia, photo courtesy of The Lighthouse People

Three loud blasts sounded from the ship's horn as it sailed past the little lighthouse with sailors on deck waving back to the girl who waved at them.

For over forty years, Florence Martus greeted each passing ship by waving a towel during the day or a lantern at night. Born at the Cockspur Island Lighthouse near Savannah, Georgia when her father was the keeper, she moved with her brother to the nearby Elba Lighthouse when he became its keeper after her parents died.

Life at the lighthouse was lonely for eighteen-year-old Florence, with no neighbors nearby and no younger siblings. However, when she began waving at ships, she discovered a way to find friends. Over the years she gained a worldwide reputation for being "The Waving Girl," from ships that passed the lighthouse on their way to the port in

Savannah, Georgia.

Letters and gifts arrived at the lighthouse to thank Florence for her warm greeting. She received fruit, plants, jewelry, exotic birds and even a llama from Peru as grateful sailors reciprocated. Anticipation replaced loneliness as Florence looked forward to welcoming each ship.

When Florence's brother retired, they moved to Savannah. On her 70th birthday, she was honored by a citywide birthday party and the unveiling of a bronze statue of The Waving Girl, which stands by the waterfront.

Florence's life echoes the wisdom of an old proverb. *"A man(person) who has friends must be friendly."* Proverbs 18:24 NKJV

Reflections

Would you like to have friends? Try being friendly to others.

Beacon Briefs

Cockspur Island, Georgia

Although the Elba Island Lighthouse no longer exists, the Cockspur Island Light, the smallest lighthouse in Georgia, still sits in the south channel of the Savannah River where it is often visited by kayakers. No longer an active aid to navigation, the lighthouse is now part of the Fort Pulaski National Monument and is not open to the public.

Fearing the Worst

Matinicus Rock Lighthouse, Maine, photo courtesy of The Lighthouse People

Shouldn't Father be back by now?" Abbie Burgess turned from the window to look at her invalid mother. Her father, the lighthouse keeper, had been gone over a week to get supplies from the mainland.

"The storm seems to be getting worse. I doubt he can make it back today," said Abbie's mother, concern creasing her brow.

The deafening roar of the wind intensified as waves crashed over the rocks, followed by sleet and snow. Water soon covered the island and began to seep in under the doors and around the windows of the keeper's house where the family lived. Abbie's little sister screamed and clung to her mother each time a wave splashed against the house. Ice cold water rose above their feet, and the women exchanged worried glances.

"We must get to the lighthouse," said Abbie, shivering with the chill of her wet clothes. She helped the others into the tower, then watched in terror from the top of the lighthouse as their home was torn apart by the raging waves. They could only hope and pray the tower would withstand the force of the storm.

For four weeks, the women remained in the lighthouse tower on Matinicus Rock off the coast of Maine, while seventeen-year-old Abbie made sure the twenty-eight lamps of the beacon stayed lit throughout the nights.

What thoughts must have raced through their minds as they waited for the storm to end and Keeper Burgess to return? Surely, they feared for his life as well as their own. Would they starve to death or drown? How long would the storm last? The year was 1856, and there was no way to communicate with the mainland, nine miles away.

Fears without, fears within. Fear can bring a sense of helplessness or despair. Or fear can lead us to place our hope in God for his protection. As Abbie Burgess wrote afterwards, "Though at times I was greatly exhausted by my labors . . . Under God I was able to perform all my duties."

"Therefore, we will not fear, Even though the earth be removed,
And though the mountains be carried into the midst of the sea" Psalm 46:2

Reflections

Are you afraid to take on a responsibility you think is too big for you? It's not too big for God, so let Him help you.

Beacon Briefs

Matinicus Rock, Maine

After years of keepers surviving the harsh elements of the Matinicus Rock Island, the lighthouse was automated in 1983. The island is now licensed to the Audubon Society for the study of shorebirds and is the southernmost nesting site for the Atlantic Puffin.

The Lighthouse Lookout

Cape Lookout, North Carolina, photo courtesy of The Lighthouse People

The keeper climbed up the darkened steps of Cape Lookout lighthouse, using a flashlight as his guide. At the top, he would join the Coast Guardsman assigned to his tower.

Normally, the light would already be lit, but tonight it would stay dark, and for many nights to come, as long as danger lurked offshore.

It was mid-April 1942, and officials had imposed a blackout on the coast, requiring all lighthouses along the Eastern seaboard, as well as all coastal cities to be kept dark. The country was at war, and although the battleground was in Europe and the Pacific, the enemy was lurking nearby, wreaking havoc just off American shores.

From January to April, Hitler's German U-Boats sank 80 ships off the coast of North Carolina's Outer Banks. Unknowingly, the lighthouses had helped them, illuminating vulnerable merchant ships to the enemy as they passed by in the dark night. Hiding below the surface, the Germans referred to their success as the "Atlantic Turkey Shoot," bragging about the ease with which they sank the ships, turning the area into Torpedo Alley.

After an alarming loss of ships in March at the rate of one a day, the United States responded by taking action. In addition to the blackout, lookouts were stationed up and down the coast to search for signs of U-boats. Lighthouses, beach towers and beach patrols from horseback were used to look for enemy boats. In addition, the water was patrolled by armed trawlers who attacked the U-boats before they could attack the American ships. Eventually, the threat was removed, and no more U.S. ships were lost on the Homefront.

The country had been caught off guard, unaware of the close presence of danger. It wasn't until tragedy struck that the threat was realized, and defensive action was taken.

People have unseen enemies as well. There is an evil in this world that tries to hurt, kill, discourage, and defeat us. Although we cannot see it, it can wreak havoc in our lives. God warned us of this enemy in 1 Peter 5:8, "Be self-controlled and alert. Your enemy the devil prowls around like a roaring lion looking for someone to devour."

But He also gave us hope to defeat this enemy in John 16:33 *"I have told you these things, so that in me you may have peace. In this world you will have trouble.*

But take heart! I have overcome the world."

Reflections

Are you in a battle? Remember that Jesus will fight for you.

Beacon Briefs

Cape Lookout, North Carolina

Cape Lookout, located on the Outer Banks, is the only lighthouse in the United States with a diamond pattern. The white diamond points east-west and the black diamonds point in a north-south direction.

A Long Walk Home

Old Saybrook Breakwater Lighthouse, Connecticut, photo courtesy of
Jeremy D'Entremont

Walking to school is not unusual. However, walking half a mile across a pile of stone rip rap in the middle of a river can be challenging.

Seven-year-old Doris McLintock made this walk each school day between her home and the mainland. She lived at the Old Saybrook Breakwater Lighthouse, built at the end of a breakwater near the mouth of the Connecticut River. Fortunately, Doris didn't have to make the trip alone. Her father always went with her to make sure she was safe and didn't fall off the wall or in between the stones.

When the weather was warm and pleasant, Doris enjoyed walking along the breakwater wall taking in the view and listening to the cry of sea gulls and the blast of ship horns.

But in the winter, chilling winds gusted across the

water, splashing waves and spray high over the wall, making the walk hazardous. On those days, going to shore was not possible. Sometimes the weather was unpredictable such as the day Doris was at school and her father came to take her home early due to the threat of an oncoming storm.

As they returned along the breakwater, the tide was already high with water crashing over the wall. Doris and her father hurried along the top, trying to dodge each wave. When they reached the middle of the breakwater, a giant wave headed straight toward them. There was no place to go. They couldn't escape. Doris's father braced himself and held her tightly as the wall of water covered them. Miraculously, they stayed on the wall.

Years later Doris was asked if she was ever afraid living in the midst of howling winds and high seas. In her book, *Dory of the Lighthouse*, she said, "I don't remember being frightened, no doubt because my father was always near."

"Yea though I walk through the valley of the shadow of death, I will fear no evil for You are with me;" Psalm 23:4 NKJV

Reflections

Do you wish you had a father to help you make it through dangerous situations? You do, you have a heavenly Father who is always with you

Beacon Briefs

Saybrook Breakwater, Connecticut

In 1938, during New England's worst hurricane, almost everything including a 1500-gallon tank of kerosene was swept away. However, the tower still stood. The keeper and his assistant were able to survive in the lighthouse and keep the light burning throughout the storm.

The Lighthouse Mail Carriers -
Snail mail, email or pmail?

Tasman Island Light, Australia, photo by Peterdownunder, courtesy of
Wikimedia Commons

The window of the Tasman Island lighthouse opened, and a dozen pigeons flew out, each with a tiny satchel attached to one leg. Each satchel contained a message. "Send help. Need doctor."

An accident had occurred at the remote lighthouse, and the only way to summon help was with homing pigeons. The keeper and his family prayed the pigeons would be strong enough to fly the 133 miles to the loft on shore and not get lost or attacked by predator birds.

From Australia to Maine to the offshore lighthouses of the Florida Reef, homing pigeons were the main means of communication for many isolated lighthouses until radios and phone lines were installed.

Used especially for emergencies, lighthouse pigeons sometimes conveyed other news – need for supplies as well as conversational messages to family members. In addition, the pigeons returned to the lighthouse with news of local or world events. In 1918, a pigeon returned to the Bird Island Lighthouse at South Africa with the announcement that World War I had ended.

"Evening, morning and noon I cry out in distress, and He hears my voice." Psalm 55:17

Reflections

Sometimes we too, feel remote from others. We wonder if anyone sees us or hears us. But God does, and He is never too far away.

Beacon Briefs

Tasman Island, Australia

With its isolated and dangerous location 700 feet above the water on sheer cliffs, Tasman Island was a very unpopular assignment for lightkeepers and their families. These days, the light is solar-powered, and the property is leased by the Australian Maritime Safety Authority. Once or twice a year, the lighthouse and island are open to the public via helicopter tours.

A Lesson in Persistence

Bell Rock Lighthouse, photo by Ian Cowe

Robert Stevenson took a deep breath and straightened his vest before entering the meeting. He expected the same response he'd received before— "no, too expensive, impossible." Still, he hoped that this time he'd convince the Board to give him authorization to build his lighthouse on Bell Rock, off the coast of Scotland. After the recent wreck of a warship where many perished, perhaps now the Board would listen to reason and prevent future tragedies.

The young Scottish engineer presented his revised proposal to the somber-faced men. When he finished, the chairman spoke. "Mr. Stevenson, we appreciate your plan, and we've decided to go forward to get the legislation through Parliament. However, due to your relative inexperience, we're going to offer the project to Mr. John Rennie, who is not only more experienced, but has a plan less costly than yours. However, we would like to hire you

151

as Mr. Rennie's assistant."

Stevenson nodded, but his heart sank. He knew his plan would work. He was the one who'd been petitioning the Board for years, not Rennie. But he wouldn't give up. He'd oversee the project and implement his own plans as he could.

The building of the Bell Rock Lighthouse finally began in 1807 with Stevenson's public prayer over the project for those employed on the construction of the Bell Rock Lighthouse. He asked God to prosper the work, and for the structure to last long after the builders did.

Because Rennie was preoccupied with projects elsewhere, he seldom visited the site, leaving Stevenson in charge of the entire construction, laborers, and supplies.

Part of Stevenson's unique plan was to build a barracks on the reef where the laborers could live instead of being brought back and forth to the reef. Until the small barracks were finished a year later, the men stayed on a ship anchored a mile away. Work could only be done from May until October due to the harsh winters, resulting in long days of labor. For the next four years, the workers suffered cramped living conditions, absence from families, danger, and numerous obstacles. Stevenson lived alongside them, sharing the same conditions. When visitors went to survey the work, they often questioned Stevenson's Spartan life. His response was that the only possession he truly needed was the Bible.

In February 1811, Bell Rock Lighthouse was lit, and Stevenson saw his persistence pay off. To bless the building, he offered this prayer. "May the Greater Architect of the Universe under whose blessing this perilous work has prospered, preserve it as a guide to the mariner."

Robert Stevenson's persistence paid off. He believed

in his plan, his ability to manage the project, and his Creator to bless his work.

"So I say to you: Ask and it will be given to you; seek and you will find; knock and the door will be opened to you. For everyone who asks receives; the one who seeks finds; and to the one who knocks, the door will be opened." Luke 11:9-10

Reflections

Do you have a plan or project that keeps facing obstacles? Don't give up, by knock on heaven's door, seek God's will and ask for help.

Beacon Briefs

Bell Rock Lighthouse, Scotland

Two-hundred-year-old Bell Rock Lighthouse off the coast of Scotland is the oldest surviving, lighthouse built in water. According to legend, the rock was so named because a 14th-century Abbot had a bell installed on it. However, a pirate stole the bell a year later. Because of the engineering challenges that were overcome to build the lighthouse, it has been described as one of the "Seven Wonders of the Industrial World."

Following in Father's Footsteps

Corsewall Lighthouse, photo by S. Hallock DuPont, Jr., courtesy of
Lighthouse Digest magazine

N o matter how hard he tried, Robert couldn't get interested in the family business. Although his grandfather, father and uncles had carried on the tradition of engineering, Robert fought the pressure to join them in the trade.

From the time of his youth, Robert had accompanied his father Thomas, sailing the sometimes turbulent seas around Scotland to build lighthouses on the coastline. The beauty of the scenery waxed poetic for young Robert, providing his imagination with settings for stories. But his desire to be an author plus his poor health removed him

155

from the hard work of lighthouse-building. The experiences on those journeys, though, were stored in his mind to be used later when he began writing. Perhaps you remember *Treasure Island*, or *Kidnapped*.

Yes, this was the author Robert Louis Stevenson, whose family was a dynasty of engineers, specializing in lighthouse building. The Stevenson family is responsible for building 97 lighthouses on the coast of Scotland, many still operating. But Robert followed a different path and became an author.

Following in a father's footsteps can mean carrying on the father's habits. Sometimes this is good, sometimes it's not, depending on the character of the earthly father. It's a choice we have to make, despite the examples we grew up with – do we follow the good habits or the bad?

Jesus said in John 6:38, *"For I have come down from heaven not to do my will but to do the will of him (my Father) who sent me."*

Reflections

Earthly fathers have faults, but our heavenly Father does not. Jesus followed the will of his father, His good and perfect will. Whose path will you follow? Following God is always a good choice.

Beacon Briefs

Corsewall Lighthouse, Scotland

Corsewall Lighthouse, one of the lighthouses built by Robert Stevenson in 1816, is now a four-star hotel. The word "coresewall" means the place or well of the cross.

Misjudging By Appearance

Robbins Reef, New York, photo courtesy of The Lighthouse People

When Keeper John Walker first arrived at Robbins Reef Light with his wife Kate, she threatened to leave him. She had not expected to live in a home surrounded by water. However, she got used to living in the lighthouse in the middle of the channel leading to New York Harbor. In fact, Kate was eventually appointed assistant lighthouse keeper, serving in that capacity until John died three years later. His last words to her were, "Mind the light, Kate."

Several men were offered the position to be John's replacement, but they all refused, saying the location was too lonely. So Kate, the forty-year-old mother of two, applied for the position. Objections were raised against her appointment due to her size, doubting she could handle a man's job. At four-foot-ten and 100 pounds, the task seemed too large for the little woman.

But Kate received the appointment and proved she was as good at the job as any man. Not only did she keep the light burning, she also rescued at least fifty people whose boats wrecked on the reef during storms. When fog rolled in, she had to go down into the basement to start the fog machine engine to send out siren blasts. Occasionally, the motor would break down and Kate had to climb to the top of the tower to bang a huge bell.

Kate continued in her position until age 73, when she retired. Her commitment to her position and diligence to the work was commemorated by the Coast Guard. Silencing her critics, Kate proved that despite her small size, she was more than capable of "minding the light."

Too often we base our perception of people on what we see, not giving them a chance to show us who they really are. How unfair it is to make these judgments.

"The Lord does not look at the things people look at. People look at the outward appearance, but the Lord looks at the heart." 1 Samuel 16:7b

Reflections

Have you ever misjudged anyone based on their appearance? Have you ever been judged that way? God is the only one capable of judging another, and He does so not by what we look like but what our heart (character) looks like.

Beacon Briefs

Robbins Reef Lighthouse, New Jersey

Kate was the sole keeper of the Robbins Reef "sparkplug" style lighthouse from 1895-1919. When the Coast Guard took over the maintenance of the lighthouse, a three-man crew was assigned to the duties that little Kate had handled by herself.

A Statue, a God, and a Lighthouse?

Colossus of Rhodes

From painting by Frantisek Kupka, 1906

The Colossus of Rhodes was one of the seven wonders of the ancient world. And it was a lighthouse.

Approximately 100 feet high, the huge statue was built to honor the mythical god Helios, Greek patron god of the sun, to celebrate the failure of Demetrius of Alexander's year-long attack against the island of Rhodes. When Demetrius abandoned his attempt to siege the island, he left much of his military equipment behind. The

163

Rhodians decided to melt down the weaponry into bronze plates which they bolted together and filled with rocks and dirt to make the statue.

Facing east where the sun rose, it supported a fire beacon either in a torch held up by an arm, a brazier on its head, or possibly even inside the head to make the eyes glow. No one knows for certain what it looked like, since it collapsed when an earthquake struck the area 56 years later.

Legend through the centuries has said the statue straddled the entrance to the Rhodes harbor. But it is unlikely the statue was built there since the harbor would have been blocked for the twelve years of construction. Plus, it would have fallen in the water instead of on land when it collapsed. The more probable location is near the present Agios-Nikolaos Lighthouse which would have given the statue a commanding position overlooking the entrance to the Rhodes harbor, much like the Statue of Liberty oversees the entrance to New York's Manhattan harbor.

The earliest records from an eyewitness of the statue are from Pliny the Elder, B.C. 26-79, who saw the broken pieces lying on the ground soon after it fell. Even then, he was amazed by its size, saying "Few people can make their arms fit around its thumbs."

The ruins lay unmoved for 800 years because an oracle advised against rebuilding the statue. Finally the pieces were sold to Arabs, who broke down the ruins even smaller and carried the bronze away to be re-melted into other items, probably lamps.

Such a humble end from such a grand debut. One has to wonder about the power of a god that falls apart when the earth moves. I'm glad my God is stronger than that, so I don't have to be.

"God is our refuge and strength, an ever-present help in trouble. Therefore, we will not fear, though the earth gives way, and the mountains fall into the heart of the sea." Psalm 46:1-2

Reflections

Where do you look for strength when your world crumbles? God is omnipotent, which means all-powerful. His strength is greater than any other possesses.

Beacon Briefs

The Colossus of Rhodes, Greece

Legend says it took 800 camels to carry the pieces of the Colossus away. The Colossus has been a favorite reference in writings for centuries. Even Shakespeare alluded to the statue in three of his works.

LIGHTHOUSE DEVOTIONS

Lighthouse Keeping
A Family Affair

Point Arena Lighthouse, California, photo courtesy of The Lighthouse
People

"Coal's here! You boys get the wheelbarrow and bring it to the house," Light keeper Willie Corbett of Little River Lighthouse in Maine instructed his three sons. "But Dad, we just finished our other chores and we're going to play a game of baseball," oldest son Myron protested, but stopped his game to help.

Coal was vital to keep their home warm during the cold Maine winter, and the delivery was the only one they'd get until the spring thaw. So Myron and his two brothers Neil and Purcell walked to the other side of the island where the lighthouse tender dumped fifty-pound sacks of coal. Back and forth the boys went from the keeper's house beside the lighthouse to the opposite shore to bring the coal across the island and unload it into the basement of the house.

167

While the boys were assigned the heavy duties, their three sisters helped their mother keep the house clean, cook and do laundry.

Everyone in the family had chores to do on the island, like light keeper families at other stations.

One of the first jobs children were allowed to do was help polish the brass in the lantern room of the lighthouse. This was an ongoing job, as dust and smoke from the burning lamps could dull the finish and get on the prisms, preventing the light from shining properly. Tedious as the job was, it was vitally important and one the district inspector scrutinized.

The lighthouse inspector also examined the keeper's house for cleanliness. At Point Arena Lighthouse in California, Keeper William Owens and his wife Cora Isabel kept their six daughters busy. Daughter Diane remembered her mother making a game out of polishing the floor. Taking an old pair of pants, she sewed a pillow in the seat and used it to wax the floor. One of the girls would sit on the seat while one of her sisters pulled her around, polishing the floor in the process.

If lightkeepers were ill or had to leave to run errands, their wives often served as unofficial assistants to tend the light.

These are just a few of the examples of how lighthouse keeper's families shared their workload. Life at lighthouse stations could be dangerous, difficult and demanding, but everyone working together was essential to the welfare and success of the lighthouse and the family.

"Two are better than one, because they have a good return for their labor: If either of them falls down, one can help the other up. But pity anyone who falls and has no one to help them up." Ecclesiastes: 4:9-10

Reflections

Sometimes we need the help of others and sometimes others need us to help them. Who can you help today?

Beacon Briefs

Point Arena Lighthouse, California

The first Point Arena lighthouse was destroyed by the 1906 earthquake that devastated San Francisco, and a new lighthouse was built on the site in 1908. The lighthouse is one of the best whale watching spots on the northern California coast. The gray whale can be spotted during its migration of the gray whale from November through May, while humpbacks can be seen throughout the year. Even killer whales and blue whales make their appearances.

A Lighthouse of "Firsts"

Navesink Twin Lights, New Jersey, photo courtesy of The Lighthouse People

The Twin Lights of Navesink, New Jersey, were built on one of the highest points of the eastern seaboard called The Highlands. The light station, consisting of two non-identical brownstone towers linked by a central keeper's quarters, rises more than 200 feet above sea level, and has been the site of many "firsts."

In 1841, the two towers of the light were the first to use Fresnel lens, the superior navigational lighting device developed in France.

In 1883, the Twin Lights was the first light station to employ the use of kerosene.

In 1898, the light station was the first to use electricity.

In 1899, Marconi demonstrated his wireless telegraph at the site, establishing the first wireless station there.

And in the 1920's and 1930's, the US Army tested

radar devices at the light station.

But perhaps the most important "first" occurred in 1893, when a group of dignitaries stood atop the hill in front of the Twin Towers to hold the first national reading of the country's new Pledge of Allegiance. As the national flag was hoisted up the 135-ft. Liberty Pole, the crowd enthusiastically listened to the words that expressed loyalty to the United States.

I pledge allegiance to the Flag of the United States of America, and to the Republic for which it stands, one Nation under God, indivisible, with liberty and justice for all.

We have many "firsts" in our own lives too—first words, first steps, first day of school. But more importantly, we should put God first.

"Seek first God's kingdom and what God wants. Then all your other needs will be met as well." Matthew 6:33 (NCV)

Reflections

What is first in your life? Do you focus more on yourself and your problems? Try focusing on God and let Him put the rest of your life in the proper order.

Beacon Briefs

Navesink Twin Lights, New Jersey

In 1898, a seven-ton lens whose lamp was run by a generator was installed in one of the towers, resulting in the brightest light in America. Nearby residents complained about the bright light saying they couldn't sleep, their chicken wouldn't lay eggs, and their cows refused to give milk.

A Lighthouse that Lasts

Sandy Hook Lighthouse, New Jersey, photo courtesy of *Lighthouse Digest* magazine

Mozart? Beethoven? Jefferson? I remember hearing about them many years ago, but I haven't heard anything about them for a while. They say "Time flies." But for me, it seems to stand still. Yet, everything around me has changed. As the oldest lighthouse in the United States, I've been in the middle of some of these changes.

Back in 1764 when I was first put into use, this place was just a colony of England. Little did I know that in a few years, I'd be in the middle of a fight between two countries when the Revolutionary War broke out, and both sides wanted me. Not without damage, I survived, yet a few years later, found myself in the middle of controversy between two states, New York and New Jersey. Finally, the federal government took over my care.

Yes, in all this time I'm still here, looking a bit out of place in this new world. Thanks to some new paint, I still look pretty good. But I've had some setbacks when my old parts had to be replaced. Gears rusted, wood rotted, and lenses broke. You could say I'm still the same old lighthouse, but my insides are new.

Another year older? Ha! I'm not concerned. I'm still the same Sandy Hook Lighthouse, but I've been renewed and am even better than I was before. Isn't it nice to know that even an old lighthouse can have new life? I hear people can have new life too.

"Therefore, if anyone is in Christ, he is a new creation; old things have passed away; behold, all things have become new." 2 Corinthians 5:17

Reflections

You can become a new person no matter how old you are. Are you ready to let go of the mistakes of your past? Wouldn't you like to start over again?

Beacon Briefs

Sandy Hook Lighthouse, New Jersey

Stone mason Isaac Conro built Sandy Hook with "rubblestone," natural, uncut stone perfectly fitted together. In 1852, Congress described his work as one of the best-built lighthouses of the approximately 350 in the country at the time. In fact, the lighthouse was so well constructed that during the Revolutionary War, cannon balls practically danced off the structure leaving no damage.

A Soldier's Lighthouse Christmas

Cape Bonavista Lighthouse, Newfoundland, photo courtesy of Annlynn Ward

December, 1943

Private William Duval shivered as he rubbed his hands together over the small stove heater in his barracks. Despite sharing a room with 19 other guys, the room never warmed up.

Some of the guys didn't mind the cold so much. But back home in Louisiana, it never got as cold as here in Newfoundland. Why couldn't he have been sent somewhere warm?

But then again, he could be in the Pacific Islands right where a lot of fighting was going on. Guess he should be thankful he wasn't sent there. Who would've thought he'd end up in Canada, on a US base built to protect the northern coastline from German invasion?

He glanced at his girlfriend's photo thumbtacked to the wall over his bunk. Christmas was only weeks away, and what he wouldn't give to spend it with Angela back home. Home where it was warm, where family and friends gathered together for food and fun. In his mind, he could see them going around singing Christmas carols to their neighbors. If only the war would end before Christmas. But chances were slim with all the heavy fighting going on. A guy could hope, couldn't he?

His buddy Pete came in, bringing with him a blast of frosty air. "Billy! We've been invited to the lighthouse for Christmas. Wanna go?"

"The lighthouse? What would we do at a lighthouse?"

"A big family lives there and invites folks from the area to come over for Christmas. Sounds good to me!"

"Well, it's gotta beat staying in this barn. Sure, I'll go."

When Christmas day arrived, Billy and a bunch of other soldiers climbed into an Army truck. Plowing through deep snow, the truck reached the end of Cape Bonavista where a white lighthouse with vertical red stripes gleamed in the sunlight. Inside the keeper's house, an array of tantalizing aromas drew Billy toward a table laden with food. Platters of sliced meats and bowls of steaming vegetables filled one table, while trays of Christmas cookies, towering cakes, and golden-crusted pies covered another.

A teenage girl ran up and introduced herself as one of Lightkeeper Hubert Abbott's eleven children. Soon Billy's stomach was full of Christmas dinner. Afterwards, he joined in the singing as everyone gathered around the family parlor while a man played Christmas carols on an accordion. After singing, the folks played games, just like they did back home. As daylight began to dwindle over the Atlantic Ocean, Billy thanked his hosts as he said goodbye.

"We're glad you came, Billy," Mr. Abbott said. "We're all part of God's family, and what better time for a family to be together than Christmas?"

Billy didn't get to go home for the holidays, but thanks to the Abbotts, he didn't spend the holiday alone.

Holidays can be a lonely time for people separated from their families. God wants us to reach out to others, not just at Christmas, but all year long.

"For I was hungry, and you gave me something to eat, I was thirsty, and you gave me something to drink, I was a stranger and you invited me in," Matthew 25:35

Reflections

Have you ever been lonely? Who can you invite to share a holiday or a meal with so neither of you will be lonely?

Beacon Briefs

Cape Bonavista, Newfoundland

The red and white revolving light of Cape Bonavista Lighthouse was recommended by the firm of Robert Stevenson and Son and had formerly been used in the Bell Rock Light in Scotland. The lighthouse was declared a national historic sight in 1970. Today, guides dressed in period costumes lead visitors throughout the house and up the steps of the tower where they can witness a rare site: a working set of lamps and reflectors that is powered by a clockwork mechanism.

An Unexpected Feast

Thanksgiving Eve, 1888

*W*ould the gale ever end?

Keeper William C. Williams felt the tall tower of the lighthouse shake as the wind and the waves crashed against it.

Will we survive?

The storm had been raging for three days, forcing the lighthouse keeper and his two assistants to remain in the tower for protection.

Tomorrow was Thanksgiving, but the holiday looked bleak. Their families had been sent to the mainland and wouldn't be able to reunite with the men for the annual feast. Stranded on the island, the keepers watched their provisions diminish, unable to leave the island to go buy more.

There'd be no turkey, just boiled potatoes and bread. Again.

A loud noise resounded throughout the building as something crashed into the tower. Hoping none of the lantern windows had broken, Keeper Williams went up to check.

There, lying on the balcony surrounding the lantern room, were eight black ducks, dead from flying into the glass.

The next day, as calm returned to the sea, the three lighthouse keepers sat down for Thanksgiving dinner and gave thanks for keeping them safe through the storm and for the duck dinner God had supplied.

"Therefore I tell you, do not worry about your life, what you will eat or drink; or about your body, what you will wear. Is not life more than food, and the body more than clothes? Look at the birds of the air; they do not sow or reap or store away in barns, and yet your heavenly Father feeds them. Are you not much more valuable than they?" Matthew 6:25-26

Reflections

Are you a worrier? Turn your concerns over to God. He knows what you need, and He'll supply it if you trust Him.

Beacon Briefs

Boon Island Lighthouse, Maine

The 133-foot Boone Island lighthouse is the tallest lighthouse in Maine and New England. One of the most dangerous places to live, the island was hit by a severe blizzard in 1978 that damaged the lighthouse and swept away the keepers' quarters and all other outbuildings. As a result, the lighthouse was fully automated in 1980.

ℒetting the ℒight Shine

Grand Turk Lighthouse, photo of Turks and Caicos National Museum,
courtesy of *Lighthouse Digest* magazine

W here's the lighthouse?' The captain of the ship bound for Grand Turk Island searched the horizon.

"Our chart says there should be one around here somewhere." The first mate pointed to the nautical map in his hands.

A scraping sound sent alarm through the men as the ship came to a grinding halt. They were stuck on a reef, like hundreds of other ships before them. As waves crashed over the side of the stricken boat, the vessel broke apart, its cargo exposed.

Soon the ship was surrounded by smaller boats whose crews fought each other for possession of the wrecked boat's contents before it sank below the surface of the sea.

They were wreckers, islanders who took advantage of hapless ships who fell victim to the reefs.

But where was the lighthouse which would have

187

warned them? It was there, but unseen by the unfortunate ship. Something was amiss.

Back in 1852, the islands were under British rule, so shippers and American fisheries appealed to the government to build a lighthouse on Grand Turk Island. But wrecks were still so numerous that shippers began refusing to travel to the Caicos Islands for the salt mined there, an ingredient essential to New England fisheries. As a result, the island economy was hurt.

Even though a keeper was hired to light the beacon, he didn't remain all night to maintain the light and make sure it stayed on. Even when a fulltime keeper was hired and a keeper's house was built, mariners still complained that the light was not visible. The problem persisted after brighter lamps were installed. Why was this happening?

Turns out, the local keepers sympathized with the wreckers, perhaps even receiving part of the loot from the wrecked ships. So even though they lit the beacon as they were paid to do, they covered the windows with material that hampered the light's beam, rendering it ineffective. When the lighthouse was automated with no need for a keeper, the problem ended.

In Matthew 5:14-15, Jesus told his followers *"You are the light of the world. A town built on a hill cannot be hidden. Neither do people light a lamp and put it under a bowl. Instead they put it on its stand, and it gives light to everyone in the house."*

Reflections

How do you let your light shine? How can you do that? Smile. Share good news. Lend a helping hand. Sharing with others can brighten their day.

Beacon Briefs

Grand Turk Lighthouse, Turks and Caicos

The Grand Turk lighthouse was built in England and shipped in pieces to the island where it was assembled. It is the only lighthouse in the Turks and Caicos Islands.

The Rock that Held the Lighthouse Together

Old postcard showing Dumpling Rock, Massachusetts, courtesy of
Lighthouse Digest magazine

It was September 21, 1938, and keeper of Dumpling Rock Lighthouse Octave Ponsart and his wife Emma were ready to leave on a long-awaited vacation, one they'd saved for through the lean Depression years. The suitcases packed with new clothes for the trip were in the boat that was to take them to the mainland and the car they'd just purchased.

Just as they were about to get into the boat, the wind suddenly picked up and the water became choppy. Keeper Ponsart knew better than to launch the boat in turbulent weather, so he sent the women back inside while he and the assistant keeper tried to secure the dory. Despite their efforts, the boat got away from them.

The men rushed back to the oil house and the light tower to secure everything they could. As they headed for the keeper's house, the waves had already washed over the rocks and into the first floor of the house. Keeper Ponsart told the women to go to a second-floor bedroom away from the wind. By this time, the family dog was swimming in the living room.

As the fury of the storm intensified, the occupants of the house were certain they would not survive the day. Soon waves were breaking over the house as well as the lighthouse. Gradually, pieces of the house were torn off and windows shattered. The noise was deafening, drowning out the voices of the people inside who were saying their last goodbyes.

Each wave shook the house until it was leaning. A sound "like a freight train or what an earthquake must sound like," was followed by a lengthy blast of water, then a tremendous jolt hit the house, throwing the occupants to the floor. Keeper Ponsart and Assistant Keeper Fontenot opened the bedroom door enough to see out. What they discovered was sky where the ceiling had been and a massive rock where the living room wall used to be.

The rock, torn from the island's base, had created a channel through which the water could pass unobstructed. The storm continued to batter the building, but the rock held it down and kept it and those inside from washing away.

When morning finally came and the waters receded, the people on Dumpling Rock had survived one of the most deadliest hurricanes to ever hit New England. Seamond Ponsart Roberts, daughter of Octave and Emma Ponsart said, "Mom said later when she sang the hymn "Rock of Ages," it had a new and personal meaning."

"Truly God is my rock and my salvation; He is my fortress, I will never be shaken." Psalm 62:2

Reflections

God is our rock, the fortress and anchor that holds us together. Even when the storms of life attack us, God will hold us secure. Is God your rock?

Beacon Briefs

Dumpling Rock Lighthouse, Massachusetts

Amazingly, the Ponsart family survived the 1938 hurricane, the worst to hit New England in the 20th century. The Dumpling Rock lighthouse and keeper's house was not rebuilt afterwards, and in 1942 the Coast Guard tore down the remaining structures, replacing them with a skeleton tower with a flashing green light.

Tourists at the Lighthouse

Seguin Island Light, Maine, photo courtesy of Jeremy D'Entremont

As Connie put the finishing touches on her dinner, a knock sounded at the door of the lighthouse.

Expecting her guests, she rushed to the door still wearing her apron. She opened it to find a group of tourists who wanted to see the lighthouse. Connie graciously let them in, as it was customary for strangers to show up at her door for a look at the lighthouse.

Apparently, these visitors were from the English aristocracy staying at a posh hotel across the river. With her apron on, Connie was taken for the maid as the strangers marched past her to reach the light by way of the family living quarters. Connie bit her tongue, playing a proper hostess while these strangers roamed through her house, stating their opinions of it. After all, it was part of her duty living in a lighthouse.

Lighthouses have attracted tourists as long as they've been around, so keepers and their families were accustomed to strangers showing up whenever the weather was pleasant, and the water calm enough for boating excursions. Weekends and summers brought dozens of people to the shores where lighthouses stood. Most of the time, the keepers' families enjoyed the company after months of isolation when no one ventured out. But sometimes, the visitors didn't recognize the privacy of the keepers' homes, since they were government-owned facilities, and felt they had a right to roam wherever they pleased.

At Seguin Island, tourists brought an unwelcome surprise. A lightkeeper's wife had spent the day collecting bushel of blueberries to can for the winter. She was in the midst of washing the berries when a monkey came around the corner of the house and jumped into her box of berries, eating and spitting them out. A man appeared and seeing what his monkey was doing, began to laugh, calling his friends to come see. The keeper's wife was indignant and complained, but the tourist simply picked up his monkey and headed up the tower.

At Portland Head Light, a female tourist walked in and sat down at the dining table, waiting to be served. She apparently thought the lighthouse was a restaurant.

Most of us would not appreciate such intrusions. However, in the Bible it says, "Offer hospitality to one another without grumbling." (1 Peter 4:9)

Even if their monkey eats your blueberries.

Reflections

Hospitality is defined as the friendly and generous reception and entertainment of visitors or strangers. God wants us to treat others with hospitality. He also wants us to show others 'brotherly love" and treat them as we would like to be treated. What will you do the next time a stranger comes to your door?

Beacon Briefs

Seguin Island Lighthouse, Maine

Seguin Island is one of the world's foggiest places. One year the fog signal blew for a third of the entire year – 2,734 hours. At 180 feet above sea level, the lighthouse is the highest on the Maine coast and contains the only first order Fresnel lens currently used in the state.

The Lighthouse Under the Sea?

Bishop Rock, United Kingdom, photo courtesy of Ian Cowe

t's going to be a rough one." Mr. Bromley, one of three keepers at Bishop Rock Lighthouse, looked out the window at the angry Atlantic off the coast of England.

"Graham is downstairs checking the bolts and bars on the doors. I'll go recheck the windows, make sure the shutters are tight." Keeper Johnson started out the door.

A powerful wave hit the lighthouse, which shuddered as if an earthquake had struck. The keepers reached out to steady themselves.

"Yep. Swells are coming from the southwest. We're in for a major storm."

Graham walked into the keeper's quarters, located on the sixth floor of the 160-foot lighthouse.

"You're wet." Mr. Bromley nodded at Graham, his

clothes dripping on the floor.

"Stood by the door at the wrong time." Graham removed his jacket and hung it on a peg on the wall.

After the keepers were satisfied that everything had been checked, they sat down to a game of cards. The wind howled and screamed at such magnitude that hearing each other talk was difficult. Every so often, the waves rose high enough to wash past the windows. Johnson glanced from Graham to Bromley.

"You think the waves will reach the lantern room?"

As if on cue, a wave rushed over the building, covering the entire tower. The noise was swallowed up by the sea, and the room became eerily silent. Instinctively, the keepers bowed their heads, praying the lighthouse would stand. After an interminable amount of time, which may have been only seconds or minutes, the wave passed, and the noise of the wind resumed.

A collective sigh escaped the keepers as they resumed their game, thankful to be out of the watery tomb.

It's difficult to believe that waves could rise high enough to reach the top of such a tall lighthouse. Yet, in severe storms, it occurred. Can you imagine what it felt like to be the lighthouse keepers when it happened – covered by the sea, the light and noise of the world shut out? They hoped, prayed, and trusted they would come out of the storms safely and see a peaceful day again.

"For great is your love toward me; you have delivered me from the depths, from the realm of the dead." Psalm 86:13

Reflections

What would you do if you were one of the keepers at Bishop Rock when the waves crashed over? Would you panic, be afraid the lighthouse wouldn't hold together or worry that the storm might never end? In times like those, we are truly powerless to control the situation. We too, can react the way the keepers did—hope, pray and trust that God will protect us.

Beacon Briefs

Bishop Rock Lighthouse, United Kingdom.

The difficulty of reaching Bishop Rock by boat led Trinity House, the U. K. lighthouse governing agency, to build a helipad on top of the lighthouse. Before the helipad was installed, the only way personnel could move to and from the lighthouse was via a cable attached by winches to the top at the lamp level and at the base below to boats waiting at a safe distance from the lighthouse.

MARILYN TURK

The Lighthouse Army of Two

Scituate Lighthouse, Massachusetts, photo courtesy of The Lighthouse People

War of 1812
Scituate, Massachusetts

Abigail, look! There's a British ship!" Rebecca Bates, daughter of the Scituate Lighthouse Keeper Simeon Bates pointed out the window.

Younger sister Abigail ran to Rebecca's side and saw the warship anchored outside their town. "They're sending soldiers!"

Two smaller boats filled with red-coated men headed to shore. Just three months earlier, the British had plundered and burned many ships in their harbor until they were chased away by cannon fire.

"What can we do by ourselves with Mother and Father away?"

"Timothy, run! Warn everyone in town!" Rebecca sent their younger brother out the back door.

She turned to Abigail and said, "You take the drum and I'll get my fife and we'll try to scare them away."

"But what will they do if they catch us?" Abigail followed her sister, holding the drum.

"They'll surely laugh at us, but we won't let them find us."

The two girls hid behind a stand of trees by the shore, watching the soldiers rowing towards them. Rebecca only knew four songs on the fife, so she started playing "Yankee Doodle," her favorite, while her sister accompanied her on the drum.

Louder and louder the girls played. Then the boats stopped, turned around and headed back to the ship. Apparently, they were afraid the town militia would greet them if they got any closer.

Rebecca's plan worked, and the two girls became town heroes.

The odds were against the girls – they were young, they were unarmed, they were outnumbered. Yet they were brave and did what they could to protect their home.

"Though an army besiege me, my heart will not fear; though war break out against me, even then I will be confident." Psalm 27:3-4

Reflections

We often have our own battles to fight and can feel like the odds are against us. At times like this, we can put our fear aside and trust God to fight the battle for us.

Beacon Briefs

Scituate Lighthouse, Massachusetts

Scituate's first keeper, Capt. Simeon Bates, lived at the lighthouse with his family until his death at age 99 in 1832. In the War of 1812, Bates fired cannon at a British warship.

MARILYN TURK

The Lighthouse Library

Heron Neck Lighthouse, Maine, photo courtesy of Jeremy D'Entremont

Mother, do you think the lighthouse tender will come today?" Young Anna stood at the window of the Heron Neck keeper's house.

"Anna, you've asked me that every day this week. I don't know when it will arrive, but hopefully soon, as we are getting low on some of our food supplies."

"I really hope it arrives today. I've read everything in this library box several times already."

"It's certainly nice to get a new library. I look forward to seeing what new magazines will be in it."

Father rushed inside, unbuttoning his work-soiled shirt. "Tender's approaching. Get ready for inspection." He raced to put on his clean keeper's uniform as required by the Light Service Board.

Always prepared for unexpected visits, the house was in order by the time the tender landed on the shore below the remote lighthouse. On this trip, however, the inspector didn't arrive, but their new supplies did.

Two men carried in a large wooden box, its hinged doors tightly closed, and set it down in the living room.

"Here's the old one!" Anna pointed to the box that had been in their home for several months, so it could be exchanged for the new one.

Mother opened the new box and gazed at the content of books and magazines, ranging from topics of history and science to fiction and poetry. "Let's see what we have here." She studied the list on the inside of the door. "This box just came from the Mark Island Light."

"Mother, look! *Robinson Crusoe!*" Anna held up the book. "I can read it to Toby." Anna's little brother hadn' learned to read yet.

"*Ladies Home Journal.* I'll enjoy this. And look "*Popular Mechanics.* Your father always likes to read this magazine."

Like a new Christmas gift, the library box was always welcomed with excitement. From 1876 to 1938, these portable libraries provided entertainment, enlightenment and education for households otherwise isolated from civilization.

There was one book almost every keeper's family owned though, one that stayed with them wherever they lived, the Bible. The book was an important part of the household, and a permanent source of information and inspiration. These people knew the value of the wisdom and guidance it contained and treasured it more than any other book because it was God's Word.

"All Scripture is God-breathed and is useful for teaching, rebuking, correcting and training in righteousness." 2 Timothy 3:16

Reflections

Today, many people own a Bible, perhaps more than one copy. But is it valued and revered as God's Word, or is it just part of the furniture, collecting dust on the shelf? Like the library boxes, it is a gift. But what good is a gift that is never opened?

Beacon Briefs

Heron Neck Lighthouse, Maine

Heron Neck had a famous "fog-bark" signal thanks to Nemo, a Newfoundland trained by Keeper Capt. Levi Farnham to bark at ships when the fog rolled in. Named Nemo after the famous Captain Nemo in Jules Verne's *20,000 Leagues Under the Sea*, Nemo provided an important service to ships passing by the lighthouse. Although not an "official" employee of the government, whenever the fog rolled in, Nemo faithfully trotted out to the extreme end of the island to wait and listen for ships' horns.

Acknowledgements

When I began writing a lighthouse blog years ago, I had no idea what a wonderful "club" I would be joining–the universal lighthouse lovers club. As I did research for my stories, I discovered *Lighthouse Digest Magazine.* I drooled over the beautiful photos and devoured every word of every article. What a surprise I had when my husband and I volunteered as lighthouse keepers at Little River Lighthouse in Cutler, Maine, and met the editors of the magazine, Tim Harrison and Kathleen Finnegan, in person!

Tim and Kathleen introduced us to the world of lighthouse lovers through their many associates and friends. Urged on by friends and nudged by God to put my stories into a book, Tim, who has authored several lighthouse books, and Kathy provided me with wonderful support and many photos from their vast collection. I will be forever grateful for all their help. They were friends with Bob and Sandra Shanklin, "The Lighthouse People," whom I discovered lived in my part of the world, and suggested we meet.

Sandra and I met for lunch, and when I told her about my devotional book, she offered to provide the photos from the thousands she and Bob took while visiting and photographing every lighthouse in the United States. Sadly, Bob has passed away, but his memory lives on in the many beautiful photos in this book that are from their collection.

Another wonderful source of information and photos was Jeremy D'Entremont, a lighthouse expert and host of many features on lighthouses for the American Lighthouse Foundation and the United States Lighthouse Society.

Jeremy is well-known for his books on lighthouses and the tours he conducts. He was very helpful in gathering information, as well as providing some of his own photos for this book.

Appreciation also goes out to the late Terry Pepper of the Great Lakes Lighthouse Keepers Association, Annie Potts, who wrote *Last Lights, The Hand-Wound Lighthouses of The Bahamas Islands,* and Annlynn Ware for her photo in Newfoundland.

I also want to thank Kraig Anderson of lighthousefriends.com, who provided me with much assistance in my research.

For those photos outside the United States, I've been blessed to be linked through the above contacts to the international network of lighthouse lovers such as the World Lighthouse Society, where Donna Suchomelly connected me with Scottish photographer Ian Cowe. I've also met via the Internet photographers from other countries such as Esbjorn Hillberg of the Swedish Lighthouse Society who also shared some of his photos for this book. What a thrill it's been to connect with lighthouse lovers all over world and discover their willingness to cooperate on the project. What a wonderful group of people, as caring and supportive as the lighthouses they admire.

Thank you to my dear husband, Chuck, who's helped out so much by taking on more of the responsibilities for our home and family so I had time to work. Your patience is amazing.

And above all, I thank God, who led me down this path of discovering lighthouses and the people connected to them in the past, as well as, in the present. There is no doubt He intended the association from His Word to our worldly beacons of light.

Blessings,
Marilyn Turk

I hope you've enjoyed these lighthouse stories as much as I enjoyed discovering them. If you like this book, please leave a favorable review and stay tuned because Book Two might be on the horizon!

Award-winning author Marilyn Turk writes historical and contemporary fiction flavored with suspense and romance. Marilyn also writes devotions for Daily Guideposts, Walking in Grace, and contributes to other Guideposts publications. She and her husband are lighthouse enthusiasts, have visited over 100 lighthouses and also served as volunteer lighthouse caretakers at Little River Light off the coast of Maine.

When not writing or visiting lighthouses, Marilyn enjoys walking, boating, fishing, gardening, tennis, playing with grandkids and her golden retriever.

She is a member of American Christian Fiction Writers, Faith, Hope and Love Christian Writers, Advanced Writers and Speakers Association, Word Weavers International, and the United States Lighthouse Society.

Marilyn is also the director of the Blue Lake Christian Writers Conference.

Facebook – https://www.facebook.com/marilyn.turk.9/

Twitter – @marilynturk.com

Pinterest - https://www.pinterest.com/bluewaterbayou. Website – Pathways of the Heart, https://pathwayheart.com/. Two blogs: Lighthouse blog and The Writers Path blog. Sign up for newsletter and blogs on this site. Bookbub - https://www.bookbub.com/profile/marilyn-turk

Goodreads - https://www.goodreads.com/author/show/9791210.Marilyn_Turk Amazon author page - https://www.amazon.com/Marilyn-Turk/e/B017Y76L9A

Books
Historical Series
Coastal Lights Legacy -
Rebel Light
Revealing Light
Redeeming Light
Rekindled Light

Suspicious Shores -
The Gilded Curse

Shadowed by a Spy
Seaside Strangers (coming soon)
<u>Standalone Novels</u>
Abigail's Secret
The Escape Game

Novella Collections
The Wrong Survivor in Great Lakes Lighthouse Brides
Love's Cookin' at the Cowboy Café in Crinoline
Cowboys
Between Two Worlds in Heart of the Midwife
The Christmas Gift in The Christmas Gazebo
Kaetlyn's Cup of Christmas Cheer in Misstletoe Mishaps
Railroaded in Key West
Not My Party in Never Too Late for Romance
The Old Beach House in The Waves of Romance
Book Lady of the Bayou in The Librarian's Journey
Historical Hearts

Nonfiction
Lighthouse Devotions

Printed in the USA
CPSIA information can be obtained
at www.ICGtesting.com
LVHW020246221123
764571LV00068B/385

9 781959 788820